How
Revenue
Happens.

HOW REVENUE HAPPENS.

3 STEPS TO GROWING ANY BUSINESS... EVEN YOURS.

ROBERT NICOLETTI, FOUNDER OF THE HALO FRAMEWORK

How Revenue Happens: 3 Steps to Growing any Business... even yours.

Published by HALO Publishing LLC.
www.haloforall.com

No part of this document may be reproduced or transmitted in any form or by any means (electronic, photocopying, recording or otherwise) without the prior written permission of the publisher. Please contact *hi@haloforall.com* or write to HALO Publishing LLC, 1545 W Thomas Rd, Phoenix, AZ 85015.

This publication has been compiled based on personal experience, research, and the author's opinion, but it is not intended to replace legal, financial or other professional advice or services. Every reasonable attempt has been made to provide accurate content, and the author and publisher disclaim responsibility for any errors or omissions contained herein. The samples provided are for educational and discussion purposes only. All website addresses cited were current at the time of publication. Any trademarks, service marks, product names or named features are assumed to be the property of their respective owners and are used solely for editorial reference, not endorsement.

Available from Amazon.com and other retail outlets.

Library of Congress Control Number: 2024916292

ISBN: 979-8-9907149-0-8 (Hard Cover)
ISBN: 979-8-9907149-1-5 (Paperback)
ISBN: 979-8-9907149-2-2 (eBook)

Design and creative direction by Robert Nicoletti.
Cover and interior formatting by Becky's Graphic Design®, LLC.
www.BeckysGraphicDesign.com

TO MY MOM AND DAD, FOR TEACHING ME
SUCCESS THROUGH FAILURE.

TO MY WIFE ERIN, FOR TEACHING ME
EVERYTHING ELSE.

CONTENTS

INTRODUCTION

A lot of business books start with the record-scratch, you-may-be-wondering-how-I-got-here story of the author. I'll get to my backstory, and how and why I developed the HALO method, in a bit.

I want to start with you, your story, and how *you* got here.

Whether you bought this book online, received it from a friend, or grabbed it off the bookshelf while running through an airport, I'm going to take an educated guess as to why you're reading this page. It's one or more of these—and hopefully not all of them:

- *You haven't reached the professional or personal potential you should have by now.*
- *Your employees aren't performing at the level you'd like.*
- *You feel like you need to do everything yourself if it's going to be done right.*
- *You can't tell what's working and what isn't—or why.*
- *You've got a nagging feeling (or blood-red P&L proof) that you're wasting time and money.*
- *Your sleep is terrible. . . and your energy isn't what it should be during the day.*
- *You don't have time to think clearly from 9-5, let alone plan for the long haul or an equity exit.*
- *You can envision success, but something or someone is always getting in the way.*

It doesn't take a psychic to know that entrepreneurs, executives, and employees alike are feeling more overwhelmed and overworked than ever. And in the past 20 years of running businesses and consulting, I don't remember meeting anyone who unflinchingly claimed they'd reached their full potential.

The Entrepreneur's Dilemma

Let's just say: I've been there.

If you're an entrepreneur, a business leader, or a growth-minded executive in a larger company who wants to inject entrepreneurial spirit into your enterprise, I wrote this book for you. If you've read countless business books that didn't help, or the plans didn't work in the real world, I've felt your pain.[1] If you're as unlucky as I was, and hired a consultant who almost bankrupted you with ill-considered business strategies, your next round is on me.

When I was growing up, my mother always told me, "Everyone has the same problems, just a different mailing address." I never realized how true this was until about 15 years into my career as a professional marketing and advertising executive, working with entrepreneurs and leaders from small businesses to Fortune 500 companies, coast to coast and around the world. I ended up hearing the same problems, same pain points, and same issues that plagued the inner workings of every organization.

From the outside, they all looked shiny and successful. Flawlessly working together to produce their products and services. Relentlessly convincing customers and clients to trade their hard-earned money for what they had to sell. Or so it seemed. When I popped the hood, they had the same common problems—and the majority of people would spend more energy trying to avoid the root issues than to solve them. I also learned, however, that avoidance mentality usually wasn't for lack of desire. It was about a lack of commonality and communication

---

[1] That's not to say there aren't some fantastic books out there! While this book doesn't do a deep dive into the finer points of finance, marketing, operations, HR, and other essential business topics, I've shared my favorites in Recommended Reading on page 226.

with their immediate peers, in other departments, in upper management, and throughout the organization.

Despite vast differences in education, background, socioeconomic status, gender, age, management style, temperament, and industry, there was also another throughline that tied all but a few together. They were Jacks of one trade. They'd gotten into a specific line of business because they had talent and passion for a particular niche. The founder of a biotech company who began as a scientist shuffling test tubes in a lab. The CEO of a construction company who started as a framer swinging a hammer. The surfer who started (surprise!) a surfboard company or the baker who launched a (drum roll, please. . .) bakery.

All too often, "Follow your passion" or "Find a job that you love, and you'll never work a day in your life" can be dangerous advice. Passion is great, but it will only get you so far if you don't have a systematic, analytical approach to running a company. Being an expert at building a building doesn't automatically mean you are an expert at building a business. Ditto for master pizza chefs, dentists, or computer scientists working on an AI app.

If you see yourself in that, and you've spent your career being an expert in your field while letting the business processes languish, you're not alone. Many leaders, executives, and entrepreneurs haven't had formal training in the nuances of clear communication, priority setting, or strategic and tactical planning. They're not versed in the value of marketing—let alone the way that marketing feeds sales, and sales bolsters operations, and operations assists human resources, or why they're so interconnected in how revenue happens.

It doesn't help that our educational system does a lousy job of teaching the fundamentals of how to run a business. That includes my experience of working with hundreds of MBAs from some of the most prestigious schools around the country. It's not that they can't deliver value under the right circumstances; it's that they learned in a way that prevents them from evolving, adapting to real world occurrences, and developing the emotional intelligence required to cultivate and nurture a business.

So let's do some math. In *Outliers*, Malcom Gladwell posits the 10,000-hour rule—the concept that it takes 10,000 hours of practice and experience to become an expert in a given field or skill. Now consider this: In a 2018 *Harvard Business Journal* study, they estimated that the average manager spends less than 1.75 hours a day on tasks related to his or her position. At that pace, it would take more than 14 years for someone to become an expert at their position while on the job—assuming that they're learning the right way to do their job in the first place.

Do you have time for that? I know you don't!

How Revenue Happens: HALO Works If You Work It

Anyone who has launched, owns, or is a leader in a business, has a vision of what success looks like. In the vernacular of HALO (which stands for Holistic Approach, Leveraged Outcome), we call you prophets. You see ahead, you see what the future looks like—but you have trouble seeing how to get there. There's not enough clarity. There isn't a plan. And as a result, you're not getting the performance you need. That is not your fault, but it is a signal you need to take action.

As businesspeople, revenue is our oxygen. But if you're tossing and turning at night worried about revenue, and then obsessing about it every waking hour, you're focusing on the wrong compass. The HALO method is about taking a holistic approach to what makes **REVENUE** happen.

The framework laid out in *How Revenue Happens* allows anyone to get a solid grasp on business reality—warts and all—by looking through an analytical prism rather than an anecdotal one. The three steps used to get there—Align, Plan, and Execute—will clarify your vision of success, help you identify obstacles and opportunities, and put a plan into place with your team to reach the desired end result.

STEP 01: ALIGN	STEP 02: PLAN	STEP 03: EXECUTE

The rest of this book will dive into the details of the next few images, but let's take a brief overview of two major concepts that really serve as the foundation. Even if your company has different names for the various departments and functions, the following graphic should seem familiar in principle:

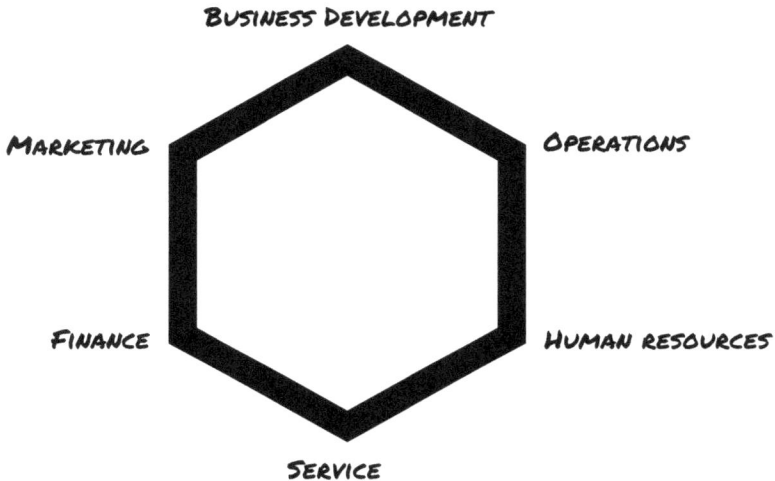

BUSINESS DEVELOPMENT

MARKETING

OPERATIONS

FINANCE

HUMAN RESOURCES

SERVICE

Figure 1: The Six Building Blocks of Business

The problem that we face today is that the majority of organizations work in silos. Unlike that nice black line, they're not actually connected—and that leads to our old friends Mrs. Overworked and Mr. Underperforming. Note that HALO is built to scale for any size business, so if you say, "Rob, I'm a solopreneur" or "I have a very small team," I need you to think a little bigger picture. Even when you contract out some of those tasks, they're part of your team. . . and if the people handling those functions are working in silos, it's up to you to connect the dots.

Assuming you're running a viable business, I guarantee they are there.

How do you bring all six of these groups together to march in the same direction? The second major concept is the 6R framework, which is the key to transitioning from an inefficient silo setup to a holistic model.

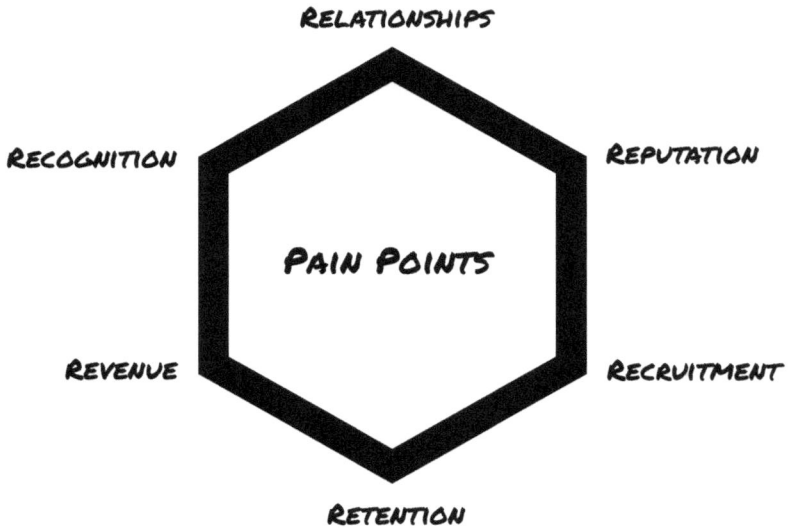

Figure 2: The 6R Framework

This illustrates the core principle of *How Revenue Happens*: All businesses have these six common pain points and building blocks—and you may notice that there are correlations between the business units in figure 1 and the HALO framework, which we call the 6R's for short. But that's not because they're the only ones responsible for them. In fact, it's exactly the opposite—it's a way of conceptualizing the common ground and creating harmony in order to break down the silos. As you work through the chapters, I will help you develop strategies and tactics to align your team, align your organization, get to that vision of success—and make **REVENUE** happen. You'll find a variety of exercises throughout the book to help you hone your approach, and additional links to deepen your knowledge.

You also might notice that both models form a hexagon, which is one of the most common shapes in nature and known for its strength in architecture. Even if you're not mechanically inclined, you'll recognize that most common nuts and bolts are hexagonal, which makes them easier to turn and apply torque, while being harder to strip. (Fun fact: Charles Darwin noted that the hexagonal honeycomb is "absolutely perfect in economizing labor and wax.")

In essence, HALO is designed to give you leverage, get everyone working together, and accelerate the progress towards your vision. Just like any program, any framework, anything at all, you get out what you put in, and that's an important piece of the HALO methodology. There's a large emphasis on accountability and follow through. Work takes work. Change takes time.

Speaking of which, you may be wondering how long it takes to implement HALO and to fix your six pain points. No kidding, I've had meetings in which people started using the vernacular of the 6R's within the first three minutes—but I'll admit that's the easy part. The rest really depends on the pace you want to take. In our online HALO Accelerator Program, for example, we spend two hours a week for six weeks, start to finish, to set up a plan. From there, it is a matter of how often you want to do review and alignment meetings to keep driving improvement. Don't worry, when all is said and done, you'll only need to apply 1% of your week to grow forward.

That said, I encourage you not to focus on the timeline at the expense of what you're trying to achieve. HALO is an evolution, not a revolution.

Failure Is a Gift

Failure and I have had an uneasy relationship over the years. With the wisdom that comes with age and experience, I've come to a conclusion: Failure is a gift.

As a college student, I cared about three things: drawing cars, hanging out with friends, and the opposite sex. The University of Arizona had plenty of the latter two, but didn't have an industrial design program. I settled on visual communication, a fancy phrase for graphic design. What I didn't learn until I was a sophomore was that there was a portfolio review to be accepted into the program. I prepared myself and my portfolio to secure one of the 21 coveted spots, confident my talents would be welcomed with open arms. I wasn't prepared for the actual result.

"This isn't for you. . . you should pick a different career path," said one professor.

"You're just not good enough," said another.

I'm trying to keep this book PG, so I won't print what came out of my mouth. But suffice it to say, at the age of 19 I hadn't experienced many setbacks outside of the occasional sports loss, bad grade, or girlfriend breakup. I certainly wasn't prepared for a failure of now-what-the-hell-am-I-supposed-to-do-with-my-life magnitude. And I wasn't about to become a geologist or physicist.

I had a choice: I could let this gut-punch failure be the anchor that held me in place, or I could use it as a sail to propel me forward. "Anchor or sail," I thought. "Maybe I should be a ship captain? Well, no. I can't read maps either."

I decided to be the sail. I sucked up my ego and camped in the hall outside of the professors' offices. Surely my natural charm would win them over.

"No," said one professor.

"No," said another.

Eventually, I found a professor named Kelley Leslie who gave my sail a puff of wind. I could audit her summer course, but it also meant accepting a major in studio art and spending my summer break in the solar oven that is Tucson in May through August. At the same time, I'd need to convince every visual communication professor for the rest of my college career to let me audit their class for credit. One "no," and I was done.

In a backwards way, this was a gift, requiring me to learn the art of negotiation— and I ran the table on securing my audit requests. I'm fiercely competitive, so learning from the corner as the outcast blew even more wind into my failure sail. I worked harder than anyone else, took on every challenge a professor threw my way, and traded my car doodles for what a younger me thought were "dope-ass logo design and advertising layouts."

Then Jackson Boelts, a professor who became my mentor, took me under his wing—by which I mean he relentlessly kicked the crap out of my work. These failures, however, taught me how to actually design for clients, brands, and the world. Jack was ruthless, which I loved. He was also the first professor who didn't make me feel like I was an outsider looking in.

Three years later I graduated, with a degree in studio art but a portfolio in visual communication. One year after graduation, I was nominated as one of the top 100 designers in the United States under 30. I didn't win, but I didn't care. It just proved that failure, with the right perspective, can turn any obstacle into an opportunity. From that point forward, I looked forward to the failure.

In the subsequent two decades, I've helped hundreds of companies and thousands of their employees to influence millions of customers and drive billions in revenue. In the process of developing HALO and becoming a holistic business consultant, I've devoured hundreds of books on business strategy, finance, operations, technology, psychology, and any other topic you can name.

Along with the successes and acquired wisdom, I still had my share of failures. I've disappointed clients, mismanaged employees, and had to do CPR on two different businesses. But here's the key: The lessons I learned during my experiences in college provided the foundation to keep pushing through.

Why do I bring up failure in a book whose central thesis is all about creating success? Because I've seen too many businesspeople living in fear of it—and that's when it becomes an anchor.

A few years back, I was working with an executive and he objected when I told his team that HALO requires learning through failure. "That's not OK with us," he said. "We don't fail." It turned out that his background was in the military, so his reaction was understandable. In his previous world, failure was a matter of life and death, not a learning opportunity. Once he understood that we were talking about failure in terms of testing, measuring, uncovering what doesn't work, and readjusting, he had a breakthrough. In reality, it's not all that different from what happens to a battle plan when you're in contact with enemy forces.

Fear of failure results in all sorts of unintended consequences. Paralysis by analysis. Stagnation. Not even wanting to try. Even worse, it takes a toll on your mental and emotional health when you're constantly in fight or flight or worrying about what ifs. You're wasting time, your most precious resource, being more afraid of what bad thing could occur than thinking about the positive results from change.

HALO can help your business overcome its most pressing problems through a proven holistic model and the critical pain points outlined in the 6R's above. It's a framework that can also transform your business through clear, actionable, and measurable execution plans, leading to predictable and sustainable growth in revenue and profitability. I designed it to be comprehensive, not complex.

Equally important, it's not like most strategic plans, where you create a 30-page manifesto that gathers dust on a shelf. One of my favorite moments since I started the company was when I walked into a client's office, and he'd hand-drawn the HALO model and 6R framework on his whiteboard. It was in plain sight as his North Star to get him, his team, and his company to their future vision of success.

I can't force you to take action. No one can. But I'm here to be your guide and coach. My goal is to help you understand that the journey is worth it, and that the HALO method's three steps and 6R framework are the way to get to where you want to be. Turn the page and let's get started.

Is HALO for You?

HALO is for you if. . .

- You're a growth-minded entrepreneur or executive.
- You can envision success but you need help getting there.
- You want to be a great leader.
- You want to build a great company.
- You want to build a great culture.
- You want to reach your potential.
- You want to smash your silos.
- You want to be data driven.

HALO is not for you if. . .

- You believe there's a shortcut to business success.
- You think data and metrics are the sole responsibility of your IT team.
- You believe plans are a waste of time because they always change anyway.
- You don't want to put in the work.
- You're not ready to be a little uncomfortable.

"CLARITY PRECEDES SUCCESS."

— ROBIN SHARMA

CHAPTER 1

PROPHET TO PROFIT:
THE VIEW FROM 30,000 TO ZERO

I want you to think of yourself as your company's Google Maps: You're at point A, and you need to get to point B. HALO provides everyone with the path they need to take: This department is going to take the highway, this one's going to take the backroads, and this one's heading over that mountain—and we're all going to end up at the same place.

But before you hit the pavement, you need to define your future vision of success, including both personal and professional aspects. What that vision is, and how you plan to achieve it, also depends on where you are in your growth stage:

- *If you're a startup, it may be a matter of formulating and honing your business and marketing plans—with plenty of experimentation, learning, and pivoting based on feedback from customers and key stakeholders.*

- *For a growth-stage company, the focus might be scaling the business by expanding the product line, entering new markets, and acquiring new customers—possibly with external funding to finance growth.*

- *At the expansion stage, you've achieved profitability, but are considering entering new markets, acquiring other businesses, or introducing new products or services. Funding is top of mind.*

- *Finally, at the maturity stage, you've achieved a stable position in the market, with an eye on optimizing operations, improving*

*efficiency, and possibly exiting the business through a sale
or merger.*

I know from my work with clients that it's not always a comfortable exercise to think about the future. It requires a bit more reflection than just thinking strictly about the day-to-day of products and services. You might feel pinned in at creating a specific vision, or that you're risking aiming too high or too low.

That's OK. It's normal. And we're going to do it anyway. Grab yourself a pen and pad, crack open a Word doc, or write in the margins here, and spend some time brainstorming on the following topic. Be as detailed as possible in creating your vision—behavioral science teaches us that being vivid about visualization makes us feel like it's actually happening and therefore more achievable.

EXERCISE #1 Formulating Your 3-Year Vision of Success

Vision of Success (VOS)

What are our most challenging obstacles?

What are our biggest opportunities?

What are our biggest pain points?

- *Recognition (Marketing)*
- *Relationships (Sales)*
- *Reputation (Operations)*
- *Recruitment (HR)*
- *Retention (Service)*
- *Revenue (Finance)*

IN 3 YEARS:

Our business:

- *What's our business model?*

- *What products/services do we offer?*
- *What geographies do we serve?*

Our people:

- *Where are we working?*
- *How are we using technology?*
- *How are we using data?*
- *What does our culture look like?*

Our revenue:

- *What is our top-line revenue?*
- *What is our bottom-line profit?*
- *How are we investing resources?*

That wasn't so bad, was it? You've taken the first step towards identifying with certainty who you are and where you want to go as an organization.

On a side note, you may be wondering why your vision should be focused on three years, not five, 10, or even 20. The reason resides in the HALO concept of evolution, not revolution. One year is sufficient for figuring out what works and what doesn't, but it isn't enough to attack bigger goals or make lasting changes. Thinking about three years is more tangible, like a bite size of the future that gives you a better, clearer vision of what you can actually achieve—and it gets you into a cycle where success breeds success. Longer than that, and you're tossing darts into the ether. It's too easy to put things off, and so much can change when you're looking at time horizons of five or more years.

Aligning Strategy and Execution

In the previous chapter, I mentioned the entrepreneur's role as a prophet. Understanding that role, along with the holistic model and the 6R's, is another key foundational concept for the HALO method.

In the HALO method, we talk in terms of 30,000 feet, 15,000 feet, and 0 feet as a way of defining how strategy and execution are related. More often than not, entrepreneurs and C-suite executives are the ones sitting at 30,000 feet; we call them prophets, because they're the ones who are supposed to see the future, whether it's 12 months or three years. The mid-level executives and managers are the ones floating in the middle altitudes, working with the entrepreneurs as well as the employees at ground level, where the work is getting executed. (Depending on your business model, that might also include partners, vendors, or freelancers.)

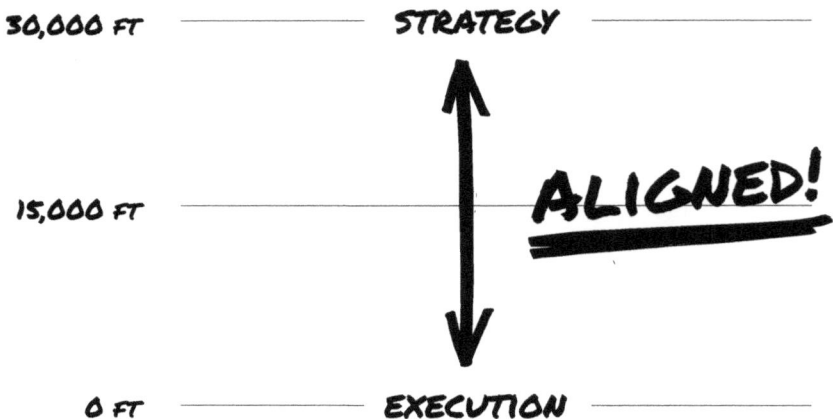

30,000 FT —————— **STRATEGY** ——————

15,000 FT —————— **ALIGNED!**

0 FT —————— **EXECUTION** ——————

To be efficient and effective, you need to connect from 30,000 feet to 0 feet, getting to the point that everyone is totally in sync about the direction of the business and what success looks like.

What happens, though, in reality for most organizations? Sometimes it's like a children's game of telephone, where the message that starts up at the top becomes complete gibberish by the time it reaches the frontline troops. In other cases, someone in the chain (frequently the entrepreneur) will have a brilliant strategy idea at 2 a.m., and share it with a few different executives or partners without communicating it holistically.

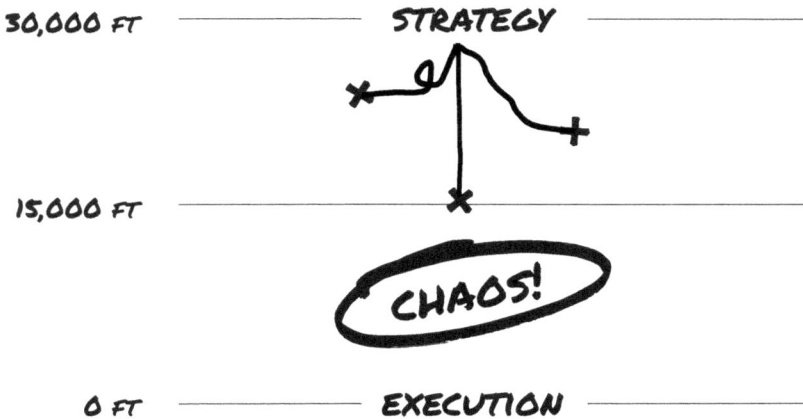

Predictably, chaos ensues from 15,000 to 0 feet. Executives, managers, and employees don't know what to do or what they're supposed to focus on. They're overworked and underperforming. They end up wasting resources—i.e., your time and your money—that you invested.

The only way to prevent that is to have a clear understanding of your current state and future vision and to communicate it throughout the organization.

Whether you're a solo entrepreneur trying to grow your business, or an internal leader trying to build your division, making the 30,000 to 0 feet process work requires that your strategic approach has three elements:

It's Clear: What's achievable and realistic? You have a clear vision of success and a holistic plan to get there, which allows clear direction for everyone below you for what they should be doing. By some estimates, employees spend 80% of their time doing things that are unrelated to meeting the objectives of the business.[2] They're managing their inbox, sitting in meetings—but that's not necessarily their fault, it's because they aren't clear about your plan to go forward. Gaining

---

2   *The Power of Clarity* by Ann Latham includes a ton of jaw-dropping statistics like this. I highly recommend it.

clarity also includes an organization-wide understanding of the 6R pain points, which we'll discuss in greater detail in a few chapters.

It's Actionable: Your holistic plan includes focused tactics that allow you and everyone in the organization to take action. The reason? Because there are only so many things that we can control, and we don't want to waste time and resources on those we can't. Sure, people still have to check emails and attend meetings, but we want to start to reduce any activities that don't deliver ROI.

It's Measurable: Your tactics use data, enabling you to track and measure performance. This is one of the biggest opportunities with HALO. It's shocking how many organizations, even large ones, have an anemic approach to data and leveraging it. Measurable success is binary—did you hit the number or not?—and it allows you to get away from finger-pointing and stick to the facts. When your team knows how they're going to be measured, they also have control over their own destinies.

Let's take the example of a results-only work environment (ROWE), an approach that was pioneered by Best Buy back in 2003 as a way to give employees more autonomy in how and where they get the job done. As the name indicates, it's all about results, and it can be very effective in the right circumstances.

Where I've seen it fall apart, however, is when companies are not clear about what results they are looking for, or why they're important to the person doing the task. I've been in far too many meetings where the executives communicate only about revenue and profit, or where the sales teams only know that they need to sell $20 million in product—without knowing how many marketing-qualified leads will drive enough sales-qualified leads to convert.

You see it all the time in professional sports. Superstar athletes like Michael Jordan and Wayne Gretzky dominated the competition for years. When they became coaches, trading in their jerseys for suits and ties, they were a bust. For all their passion, talent, and work ethic, they weren't able to translate those qualities to their teams. The results that came easy to them don't come easy to normal human beings. I don't doubt that they each had a vision of success, but the alignment of strategy and execution fell short.

Becoming an Ego-Free Prophet

We've all been in a situation where we were better at a task than someone who worked for or reported to us. It's possible you were a sales leader who was a better closer than your top sales rep, a software department head who could run circles around the best coder, or a CPA who knew more about the tax code than anyone in the building. Being a top performer is why you started or bought your business, or why you got promoted up the org chart.

Realistically, if somebody can do the job 80% of the way that you need it to be done, that might be as good as it gets—and you need to leave your ego aside. Micromanaging people or doing it yourself is also a huge opportunity cost, costing you revenue and eating away at your thinking time.

But here's why clarity and alignment are so essential for performance: If your team is just doing the job for the sake of doing it, without knowing your vision of success, it's not helpful to them or to you. The value that HALO drives is being able to get things out of your brain and into systems and processes. When you do, it gives your team the alignment they need to perform the way that you want to reach that future state.

In addition to improved performance, there's a major side benefit. It frees you up. Now you can think more strategically at 30,000 feet. You can plan for the next stage of growth. You can live your best life and do your best work.

Equally important, those benefits accrue to your employees. They're looking for purpose. The newfound clarity will give them a well-defined target.

If It's Only in Your Head, It's Not a Plan

The common factor of successful entrepreneurs comes down to having more control over their courage.[3] They need to be willing to make the hard decisions and willing to self-sacrifice. They embrace high expectations in a business environment that's inherently risky and moving super-fast. That quality is not

---

3   For more on this topic, I encourage you to check out Ryan Holiday's *Courage Is Calling*.

just limited to people who run businesses, they exist within organizations in every entrepreneurial-minded leader.

Creating and sharing a future vision of success is an act of courage. So is entrusting your team with accountability, so that they can go out and perform—ensuring that everyone gets from point A to point B.

I always ask clients if they have a plan, and they always say yes. I ask if it's written down and they always say yes. I ask if it's shared with everyone, and it's yet another yes. Then I ask to see the plan or ask their people about the plan, and without fail, there's never a plan. Leaders assume that people just know what the plan is, because it was said in some vague way at some point.

You can't download your brain, but you do need to get everything on paper so that it provides clarity and alignment for your team. If it's not written down, shared, and understood by all, it's not a plan.

It's estimated that 67% of corporate strategic plans fail.[4] In a nutshell, they don't get communicated down and nobody follows through on them. Equally stunning, an even higher percentage of executives who create those plans don't believe that they will succeed.

The running joke (and not a particularly funny one) in the business world is that a consultant is somebody you pay for an expensive PDF to tell you what to do, so that you can blame your failure on them later. HALO is the opposite. It gives you the tools to create a plan that you can implement, follow through with, and use to hold people accountable.

One of my favorite quotes—and one that's applicable to the HALO method—comes from Robin Sharma, author of *The Monk Who Sold His Ferrari*: "All change is hard at first, messy in the middle and so gorgeous at the end."

Be forewarned, the next steps of developing your plan get deeper into the hard and messy part. But I guarantee it will be worth the effort in the end.

---

4   Tanya Prive, "Why 67 Percent of Strategic Plans Fail," Inc., Oct. 23, 2020. https://www.inc.com/tanya-prive/why-67-percent-of-strategic-plans-fail.html

For a more granular look at your current and future states, head to *haloforall.com/hrh* for a form that gives you an online analysis.

STEP 1:
ALIGN

"LEADERSHIP IS ABOUT
GOING SOMEWHERE.
IF YOU AND YOUR
PEOPLE DON'T KNOW
WHERE YOU ARE GOING,
YOUR LEADERSHIP
DOESN'T MATTER."

—KEN BLANCHARD

ALIGN:
CREATE CONNECTIONS

The step-by-step formula for making connections between your business anatomy and audiences.

First, we'll address what's known in the HALO lexicon as your *ANATOMY*. We touched on this a bit in the previous chapter when you defined your *VISION OF SUCCESS*. Next, we need to identify the guiding business principles that will serve as a foundation for that success. You'll never think of vision and purpose statements or core values in the same way again, as they evolve into action-oriented form instead of static statements that don't move the needle. When you're delivering on the promises you made within your *RELATIONSHIPS*, you will further build *RECOGNITION* and drive *REVENUE*.

Next, we'll identify your *AUDIENCES*—which, in HALO lingo, has a more expansive meaning than the traditional "customers, clients, and prospects." Yes, it includes them, but we also need to identify the qualities, motivations, wants, and needs of your internal audiences, such as leadership, managers, and employees. What's inside your business matters just as much as what's on the outside.

Along the way, I'll provide several exercises to help brainstorm, develop, and solidify the concepts, so bring your whiteboard and plenty of paper. (I'll also direct you to a few links where you can access worksheets online.) Whereas you've been on your own up to this point, I recommend that you start to bring in other members of your team for this part of the process. Most DIY HALO practitioners dedicate a few hours or even a full day to each of these steps, but the timeframe and formatting of each session is up to you and the needs of your organization.

One of the challenges in today's world is that we never slow down—too often, we're at the mercy of our primitive, reactive part of the brain rather than the evolved, reflective part. While social media notifications, texts, emails, and Zoom calls aren't quite like being stalked by a saber-toothed tiger, they still set off our fight-or-flight instincts. By slowing down and working through these exercises—stopping, thinking, and reflecting—you'll actually accelerate how your business runs.

"Knowing yourself
is the beginning
of all wisdom."

— Aristotle

CHAPTER 2

ANATOMY:
DECODING YOUR DNA

Developing meaningful vision, purpose, and values
statements helps connect strategy to execution.

As human beings, about 99.6% of our DNA is the same, but it's the 0.4% that creates individual differences. The same is true of businesses, when considering competitors in your given space: Whether you're a marketing agency, a coffee shop, a homebuilder, or anything else, you've got a lot in common with other companies that do what you do. The key, though, is knowing what are the attributes in the 0.4% that make you different, and being clear about them—because people are looking for a certain type of business.

Thanks to all the time I've spent running and advising businesses, I've read countless mission, vision, and purpose statements and endless lists of company values. While some hit the mark, many of them are generic word salads that seem like an afterthought—focused on the 99.6% instead of the 0.4%.

But that doesn't mean they don't matter to your business. Quite the opposite.

As we peel away the layers of the HALO framework, I'm going to challenge you to rethink how you perceive those foundational items. More important, I'm going to teach you how to give them renewed vigor and purpose so they can strengthen your leadership and make your business more effective and efficient.

I've walked into more than a few client offices—from startups to multibillion-dollar Fortune 500 companies—and told them their mission and vision were just words in the employee handbook or on the conference room wall. Few people could recite them from memory, and nobody was living by them. There's a good possibility that's where you are too. But even if you're relatively satisfied with your company's guiding principles, I guarantee that you're leaving some critical pieces unaddressed.

In this chapter, we will examine them in a more meaningful way—and then turn them into actions. I'm going to push you to the point of clarity. What is the vision that you see? What is your purpose in the world? What are the core values that you need to live by to make it all come to fruition? When you start to put actions around these components, it creates an alignment, like birds flying in a V formation that increases speed and decreases turbulence.

Ultimately, your guiding principles impact all of the 6R's, especially your **REVENUE**. We'll discuss that a bit more after we get the blood moving with a few exercises.

EXAMINING YOUR CORPORATE ANATOMY

It's time to get out the whiteboard and scratch paper again. Within the HALO framework, understanding your corporate anatomy starts with your business model, products and services, markets and industry, geography, and business stage. If you completed the vision of success exercise from the previous chapter (or at *haloforall.com/hrh*),you've already got a good handle on your current and future states of those elements. If you haven't, what follows is a brief list of questions for you and your team to discuss your anatomical makeup. You're not necessarily looking for consensus, but rather for an open group conversation about your current and future state about each of these.

THE ANATOMY OF YOUR BUSINESS STRUCTURE

- **Business model**: Are we business-to-business (B2B), business-to-consumer (B2C), business-to-government (B2G), or direct-to-consumer (D2C), or a combination of several of the above? At some point, do we want to add one of the other models in order to unlock new opportunities?

- **Products and services**: What are we selling, both our current offerings and those that could launch within a three-year window?

- **Markets and industry**: These two words often get treated as interchangeable, but they're not. When you're talking about markets, think "Who are we selling to and what are their demographics and needs?" For industry, think "Who are we competing against with our products/services?"

- **Geography**: Where do our clients live and work? Where do we conduct operations, manufacturing, warehousing, etc.? How do we anticipate that will change in the next three years?

- **Business stage**: Are we a startup, growth-stage company, in expansion, or at maturity? What is our next step, and what will it take to get there?

While those are the bones, muscles, and organs of your anatomy, the sixth component is more like your soul: your identity itself, the aspects of your business, products, and services that make you unique, including your own human DNA as an owner or executive. The vision, purpose, and values serve a vital role: to distill them all into a usable form to guide decisions and strategies.

You may be wondering why I've omitted the traditional mission statement from the mix. In my experience, mission statements are not well suited to a holistic approach like HALO, although they can be tactically useful for specific objectives such as building **RECOGNITION** in a market. Think of it like the military, which uses missions for individual efforts within a much larger campaign; HALO approaches business operations the same way, and so should you.

VISION: WHERE ARE WE GOING?

A vision statement outlines the desired future state or ultimate goal that your company aspires to achieve—and it should reflect and encapsulate the answers you provided when formulating your vision of success on page 14. It is a forward-looking statement that paints a compelling picture of where you want to be in the long term, providing a sense of direction and serving as a source of inspiration and motivation for employees and stakeholders. It should be ambitious, maybe just out of reach at the current time, but achievable as you start to improve your processes and operations.

This is an easy one to get wrong, even for large, successful companies. I won't name names[5], but one organization I worked with had a vision that was no better than the slip of paper in a fortune cookie. Effectively, it was "We create products

---

5   Throughout the book, I have used a variety of companies, of all sizes and in different industries, to serve as examples of the principles discussed. Out of respect for the businesses and their staff members, identifying information and other facts and figures have been made anonymous.

that solve the world's biggest problems." One day, we were sitting with the entire C-suite in their corporate boardroom, and they asked me what I thought.

"Are you curing cancer?" I asked. "Solving world hunger? Fixing climate change? Or could you please tell me you're getting rid of telemarketing?"

I mean, you might argue that the vision sounded noble, in principle. And they were certainly proud of it. You saw it everywhere, on coffee mugs, computer screen backgrounds, and t-shirts.

But in addition to being too broad, and vague enough that it could apply to almost any manufacturer, there was a bigger problem: It provided no real direction for employees to drive toward. I would have preferred "ridding the world of cancer, hunger, and telemarketers," which is at least clear, actionable, and measurable, even if it had nothing to do with this client's business.

Eventually we got them to dial into a phrase that was honest, authentic, and tangible. And they accomplished that using the same exercise that we're about to work through:

EXERCISE #1	**Creating a Vision Statement that Actually Works**

One of the most effective ways to conceptualize vision statements is using Mad Libs style:

My company's goal is to help you [improve, reduce, grow, etc.] [XYZ problem] by [managing, increasing, reducing, etc] [ABC issue].

SOME ITEMS TO CONSIDER IN THE PROCESS:

- **Envision the future**: Much like the vision of success that you have already outlined,, this is about defining what you want your company to achieve in the long term and what impact it will have. Key factors to consider: What do you expect as far as growth, market presence, innovation, customer experience, and societal impact?

- **Set ambitious goals**: What are the key objectives and milestones that will lead you towards your envisioned future? These goals should be challenging, inspiring, and aligned with your purpose. They should stretch your organization and drive you to achieve greater heights.

- **Define the scope**: Does your vision statement apply to your entire organization or to specific divisions, products, or initiatives? Clarify the boundaries and context.

With that information compiled, the next step is to write three brief sample vision statements that synthesize the concepts you've identified. Some examples to help with your brainstorming:

- *Warby Parker:* "We believe that buying glasses should be easy and fun. It should leave you happy and good-looking, with money in your pocket. We also believe that everyone has the right to see."

- *Google:* "To provide access to the world's information in one click."

- *Zappos:* "To provide the best customer service possible. Deliver 'WOW' through service."

- *Avon:* "To be the company that best understands and satisfies the product, service, and self-fulfillment needs of women—globally."

PURPOSE: WHAT IS OUR FUNDAMENTAL REASON FOR EXISTENCE, BEYOND MAKING A PROFIT?

A purpose statement defines the company's broader contribution to society, the problem it aims to solve, or the value it seeks to provide. **PURPOSE** is the why behind the company's activities, and it reflects its larger impact and significance.

And, as with the vision statement, it shouldn't be something you could copy and paste onto someone else's website and it would work.

Getting this right was a huge success story for one of my clients—a seemingly minor change that has made major positive changes to their overall culture. While they had an existing mission statement, the creation of a purpose statement became (pardon the pun) more purposeful. As a construction company, this is where we landed:

"To build an environment where our clients, communities, and employee-owners prosper."

Why is it so effective? It's clear, actionable, and measurable. They tied it directly to why they exist and the value they deliver, and it moved them away from their customary focus on revenues. While they build buildings, it's not just about the physical structures, but the overall environments. Although they build for clients, the statement also reflects the needs of other key stakeholders such as communities and employees.

Finally, the word prosper is powerful and unusual in the context of construction. It cements in everyone's minds the idea that timelines will be hit, budgets will be met, and quality will be delivered. In practice, it even extended to a renewed focus on the physical and mental health of their employees.

If you're thinking, "Rob, how the heck do you measure prosperity?" I get it. But it's doable. To name just a few, we incorporated metrics for quality and timelines for clients, budgets and environmental impacts for communities, and safety, security, health, and wellness for employees. It's all there.

When you develop your purpose statement, I want you to think about each word and the impact it could have in building towards your vision of success—and your prosperity!

EXERCISE #2 Developing a Purpose Statement
that Will Help You Prosper

- **Reflect on your values**: Consider the core values that are important to you and your organization. The principles or beliefs that guide your decisions and actions serve as the foundation for your purpose statement.

- **Understand your impact**: Explore the impact you want to have on your customers, employees, stakeholders, and society as a whole. Think about the problems you aim to solve or the value you want to provide. Consider the positive change or difference you want to make through your business.

- **Define your unique offering**: Identify what sets your business apart from others. Consider your strengths, expertise, or unique approach to solving problems. Determine how your unique offering aligns with the needs and aspirations of your target audience.

Just as you did with the vision statements, the next step is to write three brief purpose statements to encapsulate your brainstormed thoughts above. Some examples to guide your process:

- *American Family Insurance:* We're dedicated to inspiring, protecting and restoring your dream.

- *J.M. Smucker:* Feeding connections that help us thrive—life tastes better together.

- *CSX:* To capitalize on the efficiency of rail transportation to serve America.

VALUES: WHAT ARE THE STANDARDS AND PRINCIPLES THAT WE OPERATE WITHIN?

VALUES statements represent the guiding principles or beliefs that shape the company's culture, behavior, and decision-making. They define the organization's ethics, norms, and the desired attitudes and behaviors of its employees. **VALUES** provide a moral compass and serve as a foundation for how the company operates and interacts with its stakeholders. Over the long haul, they ensure that your culture and systems can be replicated and scaled with integrity, even as leaders and employees come and go.

I'll frequently ask new clients if they have a set of core values, and all but the smallest companies generally have something they work with.

However, in all the times I've asked the follow-up question, "Do you track and measure your core values?" I've NEVER heard a yes. That's a huge missed opportunity. Even if your core values qualify on the first criteria of guiding principles—they're clear—they can't be effective without also being measurable and actionable. That's the only way to connect strategy to execution, giving direction to the people who are helping us reach our vision of success.

Defining and tracking your core values helps build your **REPUTATION**, because it gives you a point of leverage in your operations—the standards, practices, and principles that you're using every single day—whether you have a team of one or a team of 1,000. Every employee who works for you, every partner you know, anyone who touches the creation and delivery of your product or service needs to be adhering to this part of your anatomy.

EXERCISE #3

Defining Your Values from an Objective Perspective

When it comes to companies that have their core values truly dialed in, I can't think of a better example than Patagonia. In addition to making the best clothes in the industry, they are absolutely clear about their purpose of why they exist, and the benefits not only to you as a customer, but to Earth. They represent the pinnacle of finding and attracting like-minded people who share their values and want to interact. In short, Patagonia is about actions, not just words.[6]

In contrast, I've often seen companies resort to web searches ("Alexa, what are some great core values?"), and the result is always painfully generic. Instead, we're going to get authentic, by imagining ourselves as a fly on the wall when certain key stakeholders are chatting amongst themselves about our company without us present.

This is one of my favorite exercises with clients, because it reframes how to think about your core values. While it's a bit less structured and more freewheeling than the first two exercises, it's every bit as productive. Frankly, fly-on-the-wall is a tactic I deploy any time I need to generate an objective perspective on a situation.

In an ideal world, what adjectives and descriptions would you want them to say about your business and working with you? Take your time, and brainstorm as many ideas as you can for each of them.

If I were a fly on the wall. . .

- *I would like to hear my partners say this about working with us. . .*
- *I would like to hear my customers say this about my brand and products. . .*
- *I would like to hear my employees say this about working for our company. . .*

I often get asked how many core values a company should have, and there's no easy answer. Obviously, you can't have 25 or 50 core values, even if you generate that many words or phrases that you like. When you're packing a bag, how much do you want to carry? Not everything is going to fit, and you can't do everything.

---

6   Patagonia's core values are extensive enough that I won't list them all here, but you can check them out at https://www.patagonia.com/core-values/

Again, deciding whether something qualifies as what I call an *operational core value* comes down to whether it's measurable and actionable. Typically, I find that three to six core values strike the right balance. But that doesn't mean you should throw out the ones that just missed the cut. Keep them in your back pocket and you might find them useful at some future point.

The Top 5 Most Common Company Values—and How to Measure Them

As important as your core values are, the critical piece that many companies miss is to track and measure performance. Here are some examples of what that looks like in practice:

Teamwork

- **Employee engagement surveys**: Use surveys to assess perceptions of teamwork, including questions on collaboration, communication, and support among team members.

- **Team-based performance metrics**: Evaluate teams based on collective achievements towards shared goals, using objectives and key results (OKR's) or key performance indicators (KPIs).

- **Cross-departmental project success rates**: Measure the success rates of projects that require cross-departmental collaboration, indicating how well different units work together.

Service

- **Customer satisfaction scores (CSAT)**: Surveys to gauge customer satisfaction immediately after service interactions.

- **Net promoter score (NPS)**: Measures the likelihood of customers recommending your service, indicating overall customer loyalty and satisfaction.

- **Service resolution time**: Track the average time taken to resolve customer issues, reflecting the efficiency and responsiveness of your service.

RESPECT

- **Workplace conditions surveys**: Include questions on respect, discrimination, and inclusion to assess how respected employees feel by their peers and leadership.

- **Incident reports**: Monitor and analyze reports of disrespect, harassment, or discrimination, which indicate areas needing improvement.

- **Diversity and inclusion metrics**: Measure the diversity of your workforce and the inclusivity of your work environment, reflecting respect for different backgrounds and perspectives.

INTEGRITY

- **Ethics compliance reporting**: Track reports of ethical breaches, including conflicts of interest, corruption, or data mishandling.

- **Whistleblower reports**: The number and nature of whistleblower reports can indicate how seriously integrity is taken within the organization.

- **Integrity training completion rates**: Measure participation and completion rates of ethics and integrity training programs.

ACCOUNTABILITY

- **Performance against commitments**: Track how often individuals and teams meet their commitments and deliver on their promises.

- **Feedback loop effectiveness**: Evaluate how effectively feedback is given, received, and acted upon within the organization.

- **360-degree feedback**: Implement a 360-degree feedback system that includes self-evaluation, peer review, and supervisor review to assess accountability from multiple perspectives.

Bringing It All Together

At this point, you have several versions of your vision and purpose statements, and an extensive list of core values to draw on—and it's time to choose the winners. I don't have ESP, so I can't tell you which is best for your business, but I have a suggestion: Go through each of them again, thinking only about these three aspects:

- *Which is clearest?*
- *Which is most actionable?*
- *Which is going to be the most authentic and aligned with our anatomy?*

In the review process, you may decide that the eventual winner needs to be a hybrid of the top contestants, or even include another element that was overlooked. That's not uncommon, and in fact, it's a sign that you've been thoughtful and methodical about arriving at a conclusion.

When in doubt, remember: Revolution takes evolution.

Checks and Balances

Here's how you can make sure everything works together: Apply your final statements using this formula:

*If we measure [**VALUES**], and focus on [**PURPOSE**], we will be [**VISION**].*

ACTIONS, NOT WORDS

Creating clarity in your own values, purpose, and vision will lead to you being more efficient and effective over time. I gave a sneak peak on the 6R's in the introduction, and your guiding principles have an impact on all of them. We'll talk more about it in Section 2, but just a few examples:

- Operations, working in alignment with your guiding principles and the other five components of your anatomy, will help build your **REPUTATION**.

- When marketing is building **RECOGNITION**, they're doing it in alignment with your core values and purpose.

- Your values, purpose, and vision help you identify what internal and external **RELATIONSHIPS** are right for you over the long term, which also impacts **RECRUITMENT** and **RETENTION**.

- *Finally, when all of the other R's are in alignment, that's what makes **REVENUE** happen.*

Don't put away the whiteboard and dry erase markers quite yet. In the next chapter, we'll be doing a deep dive on the other aspect of the HALO Anatomy process: defining and aligning your internal and external audiences.

To download a fillable PDF version of the exercises
in this chapter, visit *haloforall.com/hrh*

Six Key Takeaways

1. It's not just busywork to develop your vision, purpose, and values—they help connect strategy to execution.

2. When you are formulating your guiding principles, ask yourself "Are they clear? Are they actionable? Are they measurable?" That's what makes them effective in improving your **REPUTATION**—and **REVENUE**.

3. As an entrepreneur or executive, don't forget that your own DNA has an impact on culture.

4. Your business identity is unique—you shouldn't be able to cut and paste any other company into your success formula.

5. Thinking of yourself as a fly on the wall is an excellent way to reframe your perspective.

6. Even large companies often do a poor job of the vision/purpose/values process—so use yours to create a competitive advantage!

"KNOW YOURSELF — AND KNOW YOUR AUDIENCE."

— TENNESSEE ERNIE FORD

CHAPTER 3

AUDIENCES:

ALIGNMENT, PERSONAS, AND FUNNELS—OH MY!

Three simple steps to analyze the behaviors, needs, and motivations of your customers, prospects, and partners.

RELATIONSHIPS

RECOGNITION

REPUTATION

ANATOMY

AVENUES **AUDIENCE**

REVENUE

RECRUITMENT

RETENTION

When it comes to the power of identifying your audiences, my mind immediately jumps to a telehealth client that came to us during the heart of Covid-19 in mid-2020. Like many companies—quite possibly yours—they were really struggling amidst the pandemic upheaval.

But keep in mind, they're a telehealth company, which was an industry that soared in popularity during that period. It was appealing to get virtual medical care, away from people who were infected, without having to get in a car or sit in a waiting room reading a copy of *Good Housekeeping* from 2017. Government even loosened regulations that had previously restricted telehealth companies, as far as physicians being able to deliver care outside the states where they were licensed.

As a sector, telemedicine had a serious tailwind—but this company's sails weren't catching any of it. In fact, their lack of clarity around their anatomy and the misalignment to their audiences created a proverbial anchor that was holding them back from going anywhere.

What we identified through the HALO process is that their **ANATOMY** and **AUDIENCES** weren't aligned. They were wasting a lot of resources (time and money), because the prospects who were coming through their funnel and going to the website weren't even close to being the right audiences. The organization hadn't provided clarity for their sales team, and hadn't positioned them to attract the right prospects and convert them into customers. Confusion reigned, and they were falling desperately below their revenue goals.

We started by helping them reset their anatomy, in the same ways I outlined in the previous chapter. But it was focusing on their audiences—using the processes that you'll be going through in this chapter—that turned them into one of my favorite success stories. In short, they were a telehealth provider that had a generic purpose statement about "reimagining healthcare through technology." Through these exercises, we defined their audiences as practitioners, providers, and patients—which connected seamlessly with their true purpose, which was providing access to quality care.

Here's the step-by-step on how you can get your business anatomy into alignment with your audiences too.

What Do We Mean When We Say "Audience"?

In business, there's a tendency to think of your audience as your end customer. And yes, they're part of the equation in the HALO framework, but let's broaden our perspective a bit. Here's how we break it down at the primary level:

Your 3 Key External Audiences

- **Customers or clients**: Individuals, businesses, or organizations currently paying you for products or services. Keep in mind that the buyer and user may not be the same—so you need to consider both in your analysis.

- **Partners**: Other companies or individuals with whom you form a strategic alliance or symbiotic collaboration to mutually benefit, drive, and grow each other's business.

- **Prospects**: You guessed it. . . potential future customers or partners that have shown some level of interest in your products or services. They may not know about everything that you provide—and you may not know enough about them yet either.

Obviously, those are wildly disparate segments, and there's no one-size-fits route to addressing them. But your business is nothing without them, so you need to determine a strategy for each.

Always remember: Not everyone makes decisions the same way, nor do they have the same needs, wants, or motivators. As humans, our purpose in life is to build **RELATIONSHIPS** with people, places, and things—including businesses like yours.

That means you need to look at audiences and **RELATIONSHIPS** as a two-way street, not a one-way street where you just want something from them. They're real people, and a relationship needs to be symbiotic to grow sustainably.

For that to happen, everything needs to be in alignment, from *your* anatomy and products or services to what *their* brains and hearts are telling them about taking action.

How do we create that chemical reaction in our relationship that makes them say "Yeah, I'm gonna choose you over your competitor"?

STEP #1   Analyzing Audience Alignment

AUDIENCE alignment refers to the process of ensuring that your business's strategies, messages, and offerings are effectively tailored to meet the needs, preferences, and expectations of your target audience. It involves understanding and aligning with the characteristics, behaviors, motivations, and values of the intended audience to create a strong connection and resonate with them.

As a result, we need to define who we want to align with—as far as customers, partners, and prospects—before we start thinking about strategies to reach them. In the HALO model, that depends on your type of business.

Business-to-Business (B2B)

- *What type of business fits us best?*
- *Are they startups, growth, expansion, or mature companies?*
- *Do they have a certain number of stores/employees, or revenue minimum?*
- *Who is the specific decision maker at the organization?*

Business-to-Consumer (B2C)

- *What are the attributes of our ideal customer?*
- *What are their education and income levels?*
- *Where do they live and how do we reach them?*

Business-to-Government (B2G)

- *What are the agencies that are likely users of our product/service?*

- *What are the budgetary hurdles we need to overcome?*

- *Who is the decision maker?*

Direct-to-Consumer (D2C)

- *What are the attributes of our ideal customer?*

- *What are their education and income levels?*

- *Where do they live and how do we reach them?*

So far, so good. We've got the basic "What" of your alignment as far as customers, prospects, and partners.

Now it's time to find out your "Why?"

So let's play things out in the form of a HALO grid, using the example of a company that offers computer consulting services:

PROSPECT ALIGNMENT ANALYSIS: ABC CONSULTING

	We want customers that are. . .	Because. . .
Business Model	B2B or B2C. Lifetime value, repeat business and customer retention a priority	That indicates they are stable businesses, accustomed to retainer
Business Stage	Growth	They are unlikely to have sufficient IT staff to do more than day-to-day
Business Size	11–100	Any smaller and they can't afford us; any bigger and they have large IT staff
Business Team	In the IT department, possibly marketing/sales	They are most affected by pain points of IT and data gathering

Using that basic format, you can work through your ideal prospects, partners, and customers in turn. The side benefit of this exercise is that you're gaining alignment with your team in what you believe your audiences to be.

Before we move on to the next step, however, there's another critical piece of this analysis. . .

GREEN, YELLOW, AND RED LIGHTS

Based on your past experiences at your current company and throughout your career, you have a good idea of the types of clients and partners you prefer to work with—and the ones you don't. But sometimes we let down our guard, and perhaps your team doesn't have the same clarity that you do.

- **Green lights. Ask yourself**: What are the signs that a customer, partner, or prospect would be a great fit? It could be responsiveness, willingness to follow your processes from the start, or having a partnership mentality.

- **Yellow lights. Ask yourself**: What are the signs that a customer, partner, or prospect might not be right for us? It could be that they're always asking for discounts, are poor communicators, or high maintenance.

- **Red lights. Ask yourself**: What are the signs that a customer, partner, or prospects is wrong for us? Examples could include constantly rescheduling meetings, no-showing, or constant complaining about price.

Important! Green lights are easy to fast track, but there's a major difference between yellow and red ones. Yellow lights can often be managed with a little bit of coaching and persuasion. In contrast, too many times I've seen entrepreneurs and executives chase red lights because they're hoping just to fulfill a need for revenue.

What they miss is that it's going to hurt them in the long run.

Sure, there's an exchange of money for services or products, but it will inevitably start to suck away at your resources.

STEP #2 Creating Personas to Get to "Yes" Faster

Personas are a common tool in the advertising and marketing world, and it's honestly surprising to me that it's not used more widely in other business contexts. In chapter 7, we'll look at an example of how one of the largest healthcare organizations in the US incorporated personas into their sales recruitment, but first let's talk about the concept itself.

A persona is a detailed, holistic profile that encapsulates the characteristics, behaviors, needs, and motivations of a particular group of individuals who share common traits. Businesses use them to better understand and empathize with their target customers, users, and partners—which allows them to do a better job of tailoring their products, services, and marketing strategies.

In other words: Personas make it personal.

When you create personas, you're building profiles to ensure that you're building the right **RELATIONSHIPS** with the right people and organizations. It's as close as you can get to understanding their anatomy without being inside their head or company. Personas help get us to "yes" faster, because we understand how our target audiences think, behave, and make decisions.

As with the alignment process, there are four components that you need to consider:

1. **WHO ARE THEY?**
   Clients and prospects: Age, gender, location, education, income level, occupation, and family status.
   Partners: Consider what type of business they're in, what is their title, and whether they are the decision maker.

2. **WHAT QUESTIONS DO THEY HAVE?** (Note: You should also consider what questions they don't ask but should, or what questions they might be afraid to ask.)

3. **WHAT ARE THEIR PAIN POINTS?**
   Clients and prospects: How can my product or service help solve those problems?
   Partners: How can our partnership mitigate or eliminate their pain points?

4. **WHAT DO THEY WANT?**
   Clients and prospects: How can my product or service help them get what they want?
   For partners: How can we help them succeed?
   Either: Why would they say no?

Since we used prospects in the previous exercise, let's give an example of how this would play out if we're defining a persona for partners who can help ABC Consulting expand into a new category for their services:

PARTNER PERSONA ANALYSIS: ABC CONSULTING

Who are they?	Specialists in CRM systems, which is an area that we're looking to expand into. Likely in growth or expansion stage, but mature would be OK under the right circumstances
What questions do they have?	Questions they ask: What software and hardware systems do you work on? What does the financial arrangement look like? Questions they are afraid to ask: Are you going to be competing with our IT staff or trying to poach employees or clients?
What are their pain points?	Staffing shortages, cloud migration, increasing number of competitors
What do they want?	A capable partner that not only understands software and hardware systems, but delivers exceptional service for high-end clientele

The same principles would apply if you were to perform the persona exercise on your customers/clients or prospects. If your business has multiple products or services, you might have one target audience of women between 25 and 40, and another audience of men between 50 and 70. In those cases, HALO means doing separate persona analyses of each—because you want to understand how each individual within a given category thinks, behaves, and buys in relation to your products and services.

An important caveat is that too many organizations spend all their time and resources on their customer base—so make sure you're expanding your scope beyond that. To integrate growth in your company, you need to be building **RELATIONSHIPS** with community and industry partners who can give you leverage and help influence growth through their own business.

Likewise, having a better understanding of your prospects' personas will be essential for reaching the people who are only vaguely aware of your offerings—or don't know that you exist, but need to. We live in an age in which we're exposed to about 15,000 different brands and messages every single day. Simplifying the pathway for our prospects makes it easier to work their way through our products and services.

Developing personas not only helps to improve your products and services, it will influence all of your decisions from strategy through execution. It ensures that you're staying focused.

Done right, the net effect will be that you don't have to spend as much on marketing and advertising, since you are building **RECOGNITION**, **RELATIONSHIPS**, and **REPUTATION** organically.

STEP #3   Using Funnels to Filter Out the Junk

In the same way that personas are common in the advertising and marketing world, funnels are everyday lingo in the sales realm. And, like personas, they can be used for far more than that original purpose.

You know from your own experience in business or life in general that trying to please everyone never works—and it's usually counterproductive. HALO incorporates funnels as a system of elimination, focusing your business on your essential audiences and high-performance **RELATIONSHIPS**. That protects your resources and gets you away from the toxic triad of being overwhelmed, overworked, and underperforming.

Here's how HALO incorporates the funnel principle to filter out the junk.

You'll sometimes hear this called the buyer's journey, the process of someone going from initial awareness to **RECOGNITION** to a purchase decision. In HALO, we talk about this in terms of the 3 C's: curiosity, clarity, and commitment.

But it's more than just a funnel for sales. Every company also needs to use a funnel for whittling down to the individuals that we believe are the right **RELATIONSHIPS** for us to get into. That could be prospects, clients/customers, or partners.

I'm not trying to be rude by saying that most individuals who come into our arena are junk. But remember: We're already overworked, overwhelmed, and underperforming, so we need to protect our resources—and focus only on those **RELATIONSHIPS** that can evolve into something that's long standing and profitable for everyone. By necessity, that's a process that requires paring down, and it enables us to hone our messaging based on the work we did with alignment and personas.

As you can see from the chart on the previous page, the HALO funnel has six stages, and there are fewer of each type from top to bottom:

1. **ANONYMOUS:** We don't know them, and they don't know us

2. **PROSPECT:** Contact has been made, some information collected

3. **LEAD:** Active engagement at some level

4. **OPPORTUNITY:** Meets minimum qualifications

5. **CUSTOMER/CLIENT:** Actively engaged, paying for service/product

6. **CHAMPION:** We're delivered on our promise, and they sing our praises

Yep, it's time to get out your spreadsheet. Like the alignment and persona exercises, we're going to create a HALO grid, again using our friends at ABC Consulting as an example.

FUNNEL ANALYSIS: ABC CONSULTING

Funnel Stage	Qualification	Definition
Anonymous	Unknown	May have seen website or advertising
Prospect	Name/email	Has opted in via web form; actively being marketed to
Lead	Name/email/phone/title	Has engaged with content; attended webinar
Opportunity	Name/email/phone/title/qualified	Completed our computer needs assessment
Customer/ Client	Paying for service/on retainer	Participating in our standard monthly maintenance program
Champion	High success client	Based on results, they have provided several referrals

Of course, this doesn't occur in a vacuum. The funnel also coincides with your business processes:

- **Advertising and marketing** *drive* **RECOGNITION**, *moving people from the anonymous level to prospect.*

- **Business development and sales** *drive them from prospect to lead to opportunity (using qualification, which is really where you can weed out the junk) and ultimately close the sale.*
- *Once they become a client, customer, or partner,* **operations** *delivers on the promise—with the best of the best being driven into the champion category.*

I don't care if you're B2B, B2C, B2G, or D2C, these funnels are applicable at every stage, in organizations of any size. It doesn't matter if you're a solopreneur or a multibillion-dollar company. As human beings, we all have a buyer's journey—stages that we go through to make a decision.

The goal is to use your funnel to reduce the resources, time, and money that it takes to reach your vision of success. The more measurable and actionable your funnel is, the more efficient and effective it's going to be.

Need to Refine Your Vision and Anatomy?

In the process of defining their audiences, many HALO clients find that they also need to make tweaks to their anatomy, vision, and sometimes even core values. If you find yourself questioning prior assumptions, you're doing HALO right—because making that connection between anatomy and audiences may be a critical piece of your success, but it's not carved in stone. It's not about perfection; it's an iterative process by design. You're going to learn what works and what doesn't, so edits and alterations are part of the process.

And I'll say it again: HALO is about evolution, not revolution.

Staying on Target: How Audiences Impact Revenue

In the grand scheme of things, having a three-year vision of success isn't a long time—less than 1,000 business days. Everything you do in that time span has an action and reaction, so we need to be making the right decisions.

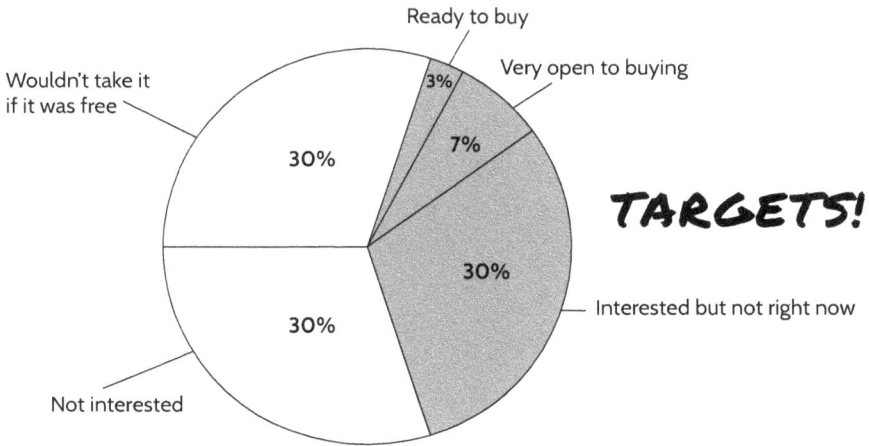

Let's say we have 100 prospects that you think might be worth building a relationship with for the possibility of future revenue.[7] But here's the reality:

- 30 of them wouldn't buy your product or service even if it were free. If you were standing on a corner handing it out, they'd walk right past you.

- 30 aren't interested. The pain point isn't acute enough, the need isn't great enough, or the price isn't right.

- 30 aren't interested right now, but might be open to it in the future. We don't know when that might be, however, so we'll need to work to stay top-of-mind.

- 7 are open to buying or ready to make a commitment.

- 3 are ready to make a decision today or buy right now.

Out of a pool of 100, only 40 are truly worth targeting. Even within that 40, only 10 of them offer an opportunity to move the needle quickly.

---

7   I learned about this concept from *The 1-Page Marketing Plan* by Allan Dib—well worth picking up a copy!

Of course, those numbers will vary depending on the buying cycle of your product or service. But every second does count in the way that we align our anatomy to our audiences, the personas we've created, and the way that we develop our funnels.

Here's the HALO way of thinking about that:

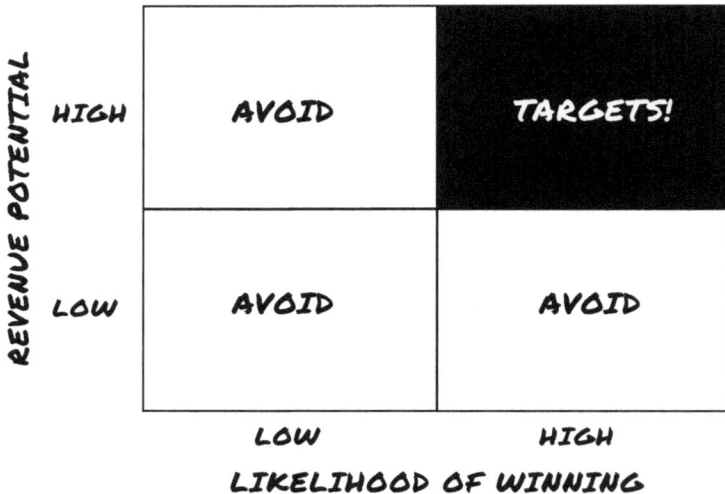

The 40 people who are worth targeting fall into that upper-right quadrant. They have high revenue potential *and* they are a good match for your products and services as defined in the three exercises above. In an upcoming chapter, we'll talk more about building **RECOGNITION** and **RELATIONSHIPS** with them, but for now, keep it simple.

One of the key precepts of HALO is to focus on the things you can control, and stop wasting resources on the things you can't. There's no better place to start than that upper-right box.

DON'T FORGET YOUR INTERNAL AUDIENCE

Within the HALO framework there's one more key audience, and it's an internal one: Your employees, the individuals helping build your business, including long-term freelancers or contractors.

I wanted to keep the focus on your external audiences in this chapter, but rest assured, you can apply modified versions of the exercises to personnel. A few examples:

- **Alignment**: What type of background, skill set, and personality will fit with our anatomy and culture? What are the green, yellow, and red lights?

- **Persona**: Based on high performers at our company, what does an ideal hire look like? How can we use that in our *RECRUITMENT* process, so that we can nurture and grow our talent base?

- **Funnel**: How can we access better candidates and weed out those who are unqualified or a poor match?

Stay tuned for more detailed discussions about employees once we get to the 6R's in section 2!

Oh, and About that Telehealth Company

I know I left you in suspense earlier. So, what ever happened to that tele-health company?

By finding the right audiences, and building *RECOGNITION* and *RELATIONSHIPS* with them, they were able to triple their revenue during the first quarter of 2021. You read that correctly: revenues were up 328% in 90 days, thanks to one simple change: clear messaging that influenced prospects' decisions, driving them from curious to committed, so that they became customers.

But hold on, it gets better. If you recall, during that economic timeframe, there was a lot of competition among companies looking for investors (who were rightfully scared out of their wits by the uncertainty of the pandemic). Partly based on their improved finances, the telehealth company was able to raise Series A round of financing, which is challenging even during economic booms. One of the investment banks gave the following feedback: The company was so clear about who they and their target audiences were, and their strategy and execution were so well aligned, that the investors were unanimous about putting money into the company.

And it gets even better. In 2022, they were acquired by a major international health care and telehealth company. Happily ever after!

Keep in mind, they accomplished all of this within 12 months. Think about that. Three months before they started working with us and implementing HALO, they weren't sure if they were going to survive, as they burned through resources, time, and money.

Make no mistake, the process was painful at times, and they busted their butts to pull it all together. HALO gives you the tools and framework, but it's not a magic wand. I'm proud to say that we're still working with them today, because they have a great company, team, and product.

Those are the kind of impact and results you can get by understanding and focusing on your audiences. That's what I want for you, and it's there for the taking when you put in the work.

Which brings us to our next step. In the next section, we're going to dial into the specifics of the 6R's—and start assessing which of the six you need to fix most to achieve your future vision.

To download a fillable PDF version of the exercises
in this chapter, visit *haloforall.com/hrh*

Six Key Takeaways

1. Alignment is about targeting: the process of ensuring a right fit between your brand, product, or service and a specific target audience.

2. By focusing on the right **RELATIONSHIPS**, alignment helps protect your resources (time and money).

3. Creating personas is an excellent way to capture and visualize the characteristics, behaviors, needs, and motivations of a specific audience—which gets you to "Yes" faster.

4. Personas also can help you improve products and services and influence strategies and tactics when building **RELATIONSHIPS** with your audiences.

5. Funnels filter out the junk, as prospects go from initial awareness of your brand, product, or service to making a decision.

6. At each stage of the funnel process, the number of potential customers, partners, and employees narrows—making your business more efficient and effective.

STEP 2:
PLAN

"I ain't Martin
Luther King.
I don't need a dream.
I have a plan."

—Spike Lee

PLAN:
FIX YOUR SIX

Lots of companies talk about breaking down silos, but few do it. Here's how to make it happen.

Every company, organization, team, or individual I've ever encountered has the same six pain points: **RECOGNITION, RELATIONSHIPS, REPUTATION, RECRUITMENT, RETENTION**, and **REVENUE**. In HALO shorthand, we call them the 6R's and these are the building blocks of your business.

Up to this point, I've touched lightly on how your business identity connects to the 6R's of your business.

In the second step of the HALO process, it's time to do the deep dive on each of the R's. In the process, we'll determine which represent your organization's biggest pain points, obstacles, and opportunities—and therefore the places where you can leverage the largest and quickest gains.

In a traditional org chart, departments are the sole owners of the various functions. HR is in charge of recruiting, sales drives revenue, marketing focuses on brand recognition, and so on. If things are going great, they take the credit; when things go sideways, they take the blame.

That's silo thinking. The opposite of silo thinking is HALO thinking, which will give you the language, discussion format, and tools to help break them down.

In reality, every department affects and is affected by the R's that they don't "own." If you've aligned correctly, HR doing a better job of **RECRUITMENT** helps marketing build strong **RELATIONSHIPS**, which helps sales close more deals, which allows operations to impress and build **REPUTATION** with prospects, clients, and partners—all of which drives **REVENUE**. And so on.

6 Chapters, 2 Essential Tools

Remember when I emphasized being analytical vs. anecdotal in the introduction chapter? No need to hunt it down, I'll paste it right here:

> *The framework laid out in* How Revenue Happens *allows anyone to get a solid grasp on business reality—warts and all—by looking through an analytical prism rather than an anecdotal one. It will clarify your vision of success, help you identify obstacles and opportunities, and put a plan into place with your people to reach the desired end result.*

To accomplish that, we'll use the following data-gathering and discussion process. Each chapter starts with a general discussion of the specific R and how to think about its application in your business, with real-life examples to underscore the concepts. Then you'll deploy the two essential tools of the HALO process:

- **The HALO Pain Points exercise**: This should be done with your entire leadership team, division managers, etc., depending on the structure of your organization. If you're a solo business, have no fear—it's OK to talk to yourself, I do it all the time. At the end, you'll have a metric that tells you exactly where you stand in each of the 6R's and helps set focus and priorities. No more guesswork.

- **The HALO Obstacles & Opportunities exercise**: Yep, it's exactly what it sounds like: illuminating potential pitfalls and prospects that directly influence the formulation of your strategic plans. But it's not just about listing stuff that's holding you back or offers future potential—you also need to incorporate the process of how they will be tracked and measured.

Before you get going, I have to offer a couple of caveats.

It's vital to keep an open mind. Don't assume or prejudge what you think your business's pain points, obstacles, and opportunities are. Let the team exercises guide you, because you may be surprised at the results.

Equally important, one of the goals of this section is to find commonality and develop harmony. In particular, going through the pain points exercise helps break down whatever communication barriers may exist, so people can start talking about topics that they may have been reluctant to before. Since you may be treading into sensitive or uncomfortable territory (and nobody wants to be accused of being The Problem), the HALO methodology helps keep the discussion positive and objective.

These tools are about gathering data and common understanding among the disparate parts of your organization—finally breaking down those silos, for once and for all.

Above all, you're injecting empathy into the process, which helps get everyone on the same page. You'll be amazed at how often your team members have similar points of pain or obstacles in their way—and at the same time, how often they don't realize something minor for themselves is a major problem for someone else. Finally, by encouraging honest, open dialogue, you'll also uncover opportunities that you weren't previously aware of.

Based on our experiences implementing HALO, this part of the process is guaranteed to test your mettle. Bring your neighborhood's best coffee, bagels, pizza or whatever else will motivate your team to bring their A game. The good news is, once you've emerged from these six chapters, you'll be ready to focus on the next step: Choosing the R's that will move the needle most and activating them towards your vision of success.

"PRODUCTS ARE MADE IN A FACTORY. BRANDS ARE CREATED IN THE MIND."

— WALTER LANDOR

CHAPTER 4

RECOGNITION:
DO I KNOW YOU?

Moving your audiences from knowing you exist to having them care about what you do, how you do it, and why.

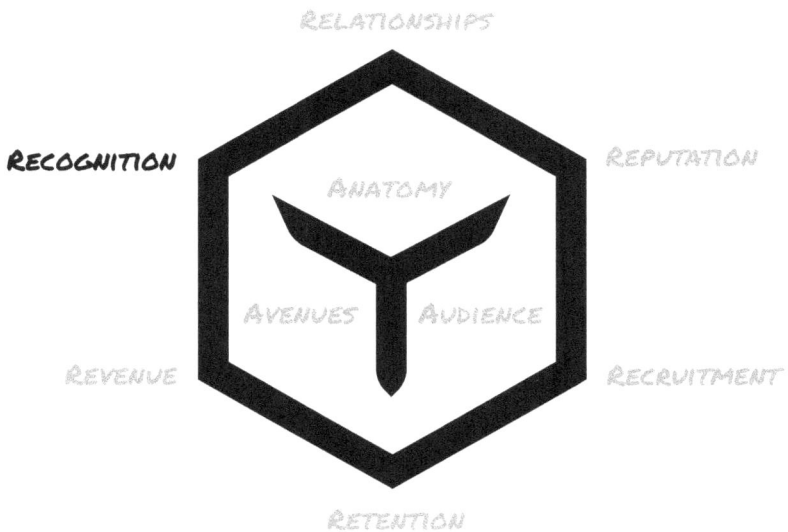

RELATIONSHIPS

RECOGNITION

REPUTATION

ANATOMY

AVENUES AUDIENCE

REVENUE

RECRUITMENT

RETENTION

To introduce the concept of the first R that we'll tackle—*RECOGNITION*—I want you to take a moment to picture your friendly (or not-so-friendly) local bank in your mind's eye. That bank has little or no control over when someone is going to leave a competitor and be ready to make a switch to their bank. Part of the problem is that banks offer very similar products and similar interest rates. They're also really sticky; it's a major hassle to move your accounts to a new institution.

Think back on the last time you changed banks. I'm going to take a wild guess and assume it was a huge pain in the neck and you had to be frustrated beyond belief to get to that point. Research shows that, on average, it takes seven screwups before most people will leave their bank. A couple of overdraft fees, an ATM that doesn't work, a check that gets lost, a loan denial, increasing fees and lower interest rates, and so on. Seven different unfortunate events before you reach your breaking point.

That's why Bank of America, Wells Fargo, Chase, and everyone else in the financial industry, big and small, spend so much money on *RECOGNITION* through marketing, advertising, and branding. In addition to promoting their products and locations, it's why they're so active and visible about sponsoring feel-good community events. They want you to have your next relationship already in mind when the inevitable happens. They want to be top of mind when you're ready to make the change so they can then be top of wallet.

In the meantime, they're circling like buzzards, waiting for a competitor to rack up their seventh mistake so they can swoop in.

Obviously, that's an extreme example of a *RECOGNITION* process that can last years. Your business cycle might be shorter or longer.

The bank methodology also runs contrary to conventional wisdom: "If I spend money on advertising and marketing, I should see an immediate uptick in sales and revenue." This might be true in your business, but banks are playing the long game. After all, it might take one screwup a year for seven years.

So let's look at the math behind what they're doing with that particular **RECOGNITION** strategy, which requires calculating or knowing the lifetime value of a customer. Imagine I'm the CEO of a small bank. I know that our average relationship with a customer is 10 years, and we make $3,000 a year off the average relationship. That gives us a lifetime value of $30,000 for an average customer. All well and good.

Now let's say our bank needs 1,000 new customers to meet our **REVENUE** goals for the next two years. It's going to take building **RECOGNITION** with hundreds of thousands of people to get to that number. How much will we be willing to pay for them and over what kind of time period? In the case of a $30,000 lifetime value, we might be willing to spend $3,000 per new customer over the next 24 months, because we know that their lifetime value is going to be 10 times that over the next decade.

No matter how long your sales cycle is, you need to know the lifetime value of a customer. Yes, I know that can be a tough piece of persuasion in a world where everyone's looking at the next quarterly report. But it's the most accurate way to understand how much money you're going to pay and for how long, and what you're going to expect from it. Understanding and addressing **RECOGNITION** is a key piece of protecting your resources, one of the foundational HALO concepts.

WHAT IS RECOGNITION?

Let's step back for a moment and define some terms. **RECOGNITION** is the ability to build external awareness for a business, its key leaders, its products and services, and its value proposition. If you think back on the funnel exercise in the previous chapter, this is at the wide part at the top: the first interaction anyone has with a business, product, or service. In terms of the HALO three C's—curiosity, clarity, and commitment—**RECOGNITION** is about initiating curiosity, but it also needs to move people to the clarity stage. Knowing that you exist is one thing; getting someone to care enough to commit is quite another.

In most cases, marketing leads the charge on building **RECOGNITION**. And, of course, you may be accomplishing this through an internal marketing team or external partners that specialize in tasks such as public relations, marketing, and advertising. You might also have a sales team that does some of the footwork, using the tools and assets that marketing creates and places using a mix of paid, earned, shared, or owned channels.

RECOGNITION for a business is built by strategically positioning the brand in front of its target audiences. It involves crafting a consistent brand message across various platforms, from traditional advertising to social media, ensuring the brand's values, purpose, products, and services resonate with the audiences—including prospects and partners.

Businesses typically look to build **RECOGNITION** in three strategic areas:

- **Industry Recognition:** An industry is the umbrella under which a large number of companies with a similar focus practice, by concentrating on the same service or developing similar products. While you may think of this first as "the competition," that's not all there is to it. Building industry **RECOGNITION** can cultivate **RELATIONSHIPS**, improve your **REPUTATION** in thought leadership or products and services, and open up opportunities for recruiting superior talent. Although **REVENUE** generation can result from building industry **RECOGNITION**, it's not the priority.

- **Market Recognition:** A market is a place where buyers and sellers meet—so it includes both the target audience composition (who they are, what they need) as well as the geographical location (where you'll find them or meet them). Building **RECOGNITION** within a market is essential for **REVENUE** generation, since that's where your buyers are congregating. As you might guess, that's why most businesses prioritize building market **RECOGNITION**.

- **Community Recognition:** Third, for businesses seeking to build their **REPUTATION** and **RELATIONSHIPS** within specific geographic areas, community **RECOGNITION** can be a vital tool. The act of building community **RECOGNITION** takes many forms, such as serving on the board of directors at a nonprofit, offering volunteer time, or donating resources. Regardless of the pursuit, the value of building community **RECOGNITION** can play a significant role in the growth of a business or the visibility of its key leaders. While it may not be a priority for all organizations, community **RECOGNITION** has grown in importance in recent years: Consumers are looking for **RELATIONSHIPS** with companies that are authentic and want to buy from brands that fit their values.

Beyond answering the question "Who are you?", building **RECOGNITION** is an essential task that is crucial for operational success and directly impacts **REVENUE** generation opportunities. Executing strategically sound **RECOGNITION** tactics generates marketing-qualified leads in the industry, market, and community in which a business is targeting. These leads, which have been qualified through marketing efforts, are now ready to receive further promotion from the business regarding its service or product through additional, tailored marketing and sales strategies. With the right strategies in place, marketing-qualified leads will convert to sales-qualified leads with predictability, fostering opportunities for **REVENUE** generation.

Keep in mind, **RECOGNITION** is a long-term play, not something that always delivers immediate ROI. (As our friends in the banking industry will attest—and as would the personal injury attorneys who post billboards and bus wraps all over town, waiting for some poor soul to crash and file a lawsuit.) While half of all your prospective customers might need your product or service at some point, less than 10% will have an immediate need when exposed to **RECOGNITION**-building tactics. Sometimes, if you're in the right place at the right time, you might introduce yourself to a connection that changes your business forever.

I consider **RECOGNITION** one of the sneaky-important items among the 6R's. It may not be an obvious pain point like **RECRUITMENT** or **RETENTION**, but it's a priority that shouldn't be overlooked. If you're entering a new market or launching a new product or service, it might be top of mind. But it can also be key that unlocks your ability to grow in existing markets or bring an underperforming product or service up to par. It's also the R that has the most direct impact on building **RELATIONSHIPS** with prospects and partners.

I could give you dozens of different statistics to illustrate the challenges we're up against in **RECOGNITION**, but I'll restrict it to a few that will get the point across. Each of us sees about 10,000 different ads every day. We interact at some level with almost 18,000 brands per day. The average person spends less than a second on each item when they're scrolling through a social feed.

As a result, your messaging requires consistency and clarity and, above all, needs to pique curiosity to have any chance of **RECOGNITION**. You need to catch people within fractions of a second, and you can't leave them wanting to try to figure out what it is that you do, or why it's important for them. Even if you do that exceptionally well, it's going to take seven to nine exposures before **RECOGNITION** starts to take hold in their brains.

WHAT METRICS SHOULD I USE TO MEASURE RECOGNITION?

For industry **RECOGNITION**, some of the most common metrics used by HALO clients include:

- *Industry rankings, either state, regional, or national (#)*
- *Industry awards, corporate or individual (#)*
- *Industry speaking opportunities (#)*
- *Media mentions (#)*

When it comes to market **RECOGNITION**, this is a solid starting place for you to build on:

- *Marketing-qualified leads (#)*
- *Website traffic for specific product or service (#,%)*
- *Newsletter/webinar/membership signups (#,%)*
- *Social media engagement on products and services (#,%)*
- *Media mentions (#)*

How do you stack up in community **RECOGNITION**? Keep a tally of:

- *Board seats (#)*
- *Community awards (#)*
- *Social media engagement on community-specific activities (#,%)*
- *Total volunteer hours (#,%)*
- *Media mentions about volunteer efforts, donations, etc. (#)*

WHERE DO YOU STAND WHEN IT COMES TO RECOGNITION?

EXERCISE #1 **Pain Scale**

First, we're going to talk about pain.

Pain points, much like physical pain, serve as an alarm system in a business, directing attention to areas that require intervention and improvement. By acknowledging and analyzing these pain points, businesses can identify underlying issues, devise strategic solutions, and enhance their overall efficiency and profitability.

That's why one of my favorite HALO tools is the pain scale, which may look familiar to you if you've ever injured yourself and ended up in a healthcare facility. In a business environment, it's the shortcut to identify the R's that need the most or the least attention.

In HALO-facilitated workshops, the process is pretty simple, and it's easily replicated within your workgroup. Hand out the following graphic and have each participant circle the face that describes their feelings about your company's current state of **RECOGNITION**. Where do you stand?

RECOGNITION

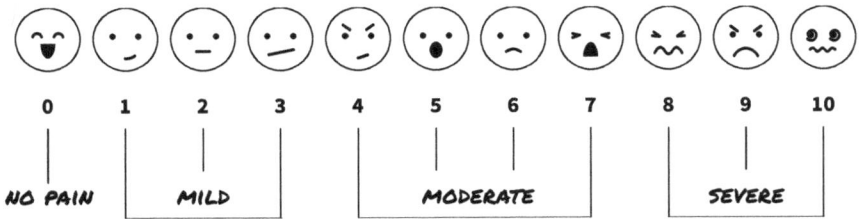

Collect the worksheets, total the numbers, average them, and enter the number in the pain scale hexagon matrix on page 179. (Have no fear, we'll get to the other five R's to complete that!)

At this point, you have two options. You can move on to the second exercise, which is a perfectly reasonable decision if the average pain scale is less than 5. During HALO-led sessions, however, we find there are two reasons you might want to use this as a jumping-off point for further discussion. First, if the average is six or higher, you might want to probe for specifics on why the pain is so acute. Second, if the opinions are widely divergent—some people have no pain at all, while the pain for others is extreme—it is worth discussing the particulars of the situation that are leading them to those opposite conclusions.

EXERCISE #2   ## Obstacles and Opportunities

My experience with hundreds of organizations in the past two-plus decades is that the lines blur between strategies and tactics to the point they're interchangeable. If you feel that way, you're in good company. And even if you don't, here's how I think about the distinction.

Strategy to me, is about two very simple questions: How am I going to increase external value to my customers, and how do I increase internal value to myself as the owner and our organization?

Tactics are about the steps you need to take. What email campaigns can increase our marketing-qualified leads? How can social media generate leads for general prospects? Where should we put our billboards? In general, most of us are more comfortable with tactics, because it feels like we're actually doing something.

Going into this second exercise, the goal is to identify what I call the "HALO bookends": your 30,000-foot strategic objective and the metrics you're going to use to measure your success. Identifying obstacles and opportunities helps identify a clear roadmap for businesses, illuminating potential pitfalls and prospects that directly influence the formulation of strategic plans. This proactive approach aids in focusing resources effectively, enhancing executions, and fostering sustainable growth by navigating obstacles and leveraging opportunities.

The Obstacles/Opportunities process will help fill in the actions and tactics to link them together. Here's how it works.

OBSTACLES

What is standing in the way of building the **RECOGNITION** needed to grow our business?

List
- Example: Time, Money, Talent, Experience. . .

OPPORTUNITIES

What specific opportunities will help build **RECOGNITION** for our business?

List
- Example: Advertising, Public Relations, Events, Social Media, Video

If history is a guide, this second exercise will spark an active discussion in your HALO group!

RECOGNITION IN THE REAL WORLD: WEEDING OUT THE FREELOADERS

I started this chapter talking about banks, which are pretty freewheeling with their **RECOGNITION** dollars—but that's not the reality for most businesses. I recently did some consultation with an amazing business owner who's in the early stages of her podcast and webinars. She'd been spending a few thousand dollars on online advertising for these courses and having pretty solid success in getting people to attend her free version of the webinar: as many as 8,000 listeners! When it came to the conversion rate, however, only about 100 of those people were willing to sign up for the paid version of the course, which costs $1,500.

Looking at the positive, she was building tremendous **RECOGNITION**. Specifically, in the HALO curiosity>clarity>commitment cycle, she was doing great on driving curiosity. But the negative is that she was also polluting her database, spending a significant amount on people who were never going to swipe their credit card no matter what she did or offered.

In such a circumstance, how do you improve the conversion rate? One option is to prequalify people, so that only 800 show up instead of 8,000. Now, if she can convert 100 of them, as higher-likelihood buyers, she becomes far more profitable. Ideally, our target was to spend $10,000 to get 800 attendees rather than $50,000 to get 8,000. This is also important when you consider how **RECOGNITION** connects to **REVENUE**: She was losing nearly a third of her income to building **RECOGNITION** in a market that was never going to make a commitment.

Instead of focusing so much on the curiosity stage, she needed to get to the clarity point earlier—before they even signed up for the free seminar. All it took was two simple tweaks: First, charging a small fee for the formerly free intro webinar. Second, doing a better job of letting prospects know before they got on the call that the cost of truly solving the pain point was going to be $1,500. And sure enough, getting the numbers in line helped drive top-line revenue and bottom-line profitability.

It can seem scary to lose people out of your database, but the fact is that it's not even worth maintaining a bunch of people who are unlikely to buy. During the funnel exercise in chapter 3, I discussed the concept that only 40 out of 100 prospects might truly be worth being targeted and nurtured over time. If you're giving away something for free, you're gonna have a lot of takers, which might dilute those numbers even further.

If you're feeling uncomfortable about the idea of charging for something that used to be free, here's another data point. There was a study done in which a seminar was offered—same topic, building, and day—but in two different rooms. The first group had paid $500 for the daylong session, while it was free for the second group.

Although the content was identical for both cohorts, the group that paid gave high ratings to the session, while the free folks gave lower marks. It's the perception of value or the implied value that made the difference.

And that's why I can't possibly emphasize this enough: *Building* **RECOGNITION** *for* **RECOGNITION'S** *stake is wasting your resources.* Building **RECOGNITION** with the right audience to have the right relationship is what drives top-line revenue, and it also helps with your bottom-line profitability.

PRO TIP FROM AN EX-AD EXEC

Since marketing and advertising are going to be the linchpins of your **RECOGNITION** efforts, I'm going to give you some insider knowledge to increase your effectiveness, whether you're working with an agency or trying to direct an internal marketing team. As the owner of an agency, and even dating back to my days on the front lines in various staff positions, it was enormously frustrating when a client wasn't clear about their objectives. There's not much you can do with a few random ideas scrawled on a cocktail napkin.

Here's the problem: When clients or companies don't have a clear, measurable, and actionable plan, their agencies or internal departments are forced to spend a lot of time guessing. Six months or a year and tens or hundreds of thousands of wasted fees later, there's little or nothing to show for it.

For you, my fellow HALOer, that starts to change now.

If I were your internal marketing department or ad agency and could wave a magic wand, these are the types of specifics I would want to hear during the conversation:

- *"I want to build **RECOGNITION** for this product in this specific market with this specific audience."*
- *"Here's what we're going to measure and the results I'm expecting: website traffic increase of XX% and social channel engagement up by YY%."*
- *"We will increase our subscriptions for this service by ZZ%."*
- *"Above all, my primary goal I want to shoot for is to drive 5,000 marketing qualified leads over the course of the next year."*

HALO tools are designed to clarify your thinking and your communication. You can dial in who is accountable for building **RECOGNITION**—for example, your head of marketing, with contributors such as an outside agency. You'll have clarity on the metrics that will define success, and what cadence you're using for tracking performance. Best of all, you'll capture time back and protect your resources, your money, and your team.

Not every executive or entrepreneur is going to be a master of each of the building blocks of a business. When it comes to marketing, you'll benefit from being familiar in conceptual terms with common tactics such as paid advertisements, pay-per-click social media advertising, and public relations and earned media.[8] But as human beings, we have an intuitive understanding of **RECOGNITION**—even if you don't know the ins and outs of marketing.

RECOGNITION is not the sole responsibility of your marketing team as they trumpet the virtues of specific products and services, it's about the strategic positioning of your brand in front of the target audiences and prospects you've identified. How do we connect our anatomy to these audiences? Yes, square one is having them know we exist in the first place. But the far more important element is having them actually care about what we do, how we do it, and why we do it. That's why it's so vital to identify your vision, purpose, and core values.

To download a fillable PDF version of the exercises
in this chapter, visit *haloforall.com/hrh*

---

8   In the Recommended Reading section on page 226, I've provided a few books that can help shore up
your marketing knowledge if you need it!

Six Key Takeaways

1. **REVENUE** happens when you build external awareness (**RECOGNITION**) for a business, its key leaders, its products and services, and its value proposition.

2. Achieving **RECOGNITION** requires clarity on the metrics that will define success and the cadence you're using for tracking performance.

3. Although marketing may be leading your **RECOGNITION** efforts, everyone plays a role in how your brand is represented to your audiences.

4. Marketing messaging requires consistency and clarity to have any chance of **RECOGNITION**—and you need to make it happen in fractions of a second.

5. Tactics will get you nowhere without a 30,000-foot strategy and metrics.

6. Building **RECOGNITION** for **RECOGNITION'S** stake is wasting your time and resources.

"Relationships are like traffic lights. I can only exist in a relationship if it's a green light."

— Taylor Swift

CHAPTER 5

RELATIONSHIPS:
THE CORNERSTONE OF BUSINESS DEVELOPMENT AND SALES

Rethinking how you build and sustain reciprocal connections with your prospects and partners.

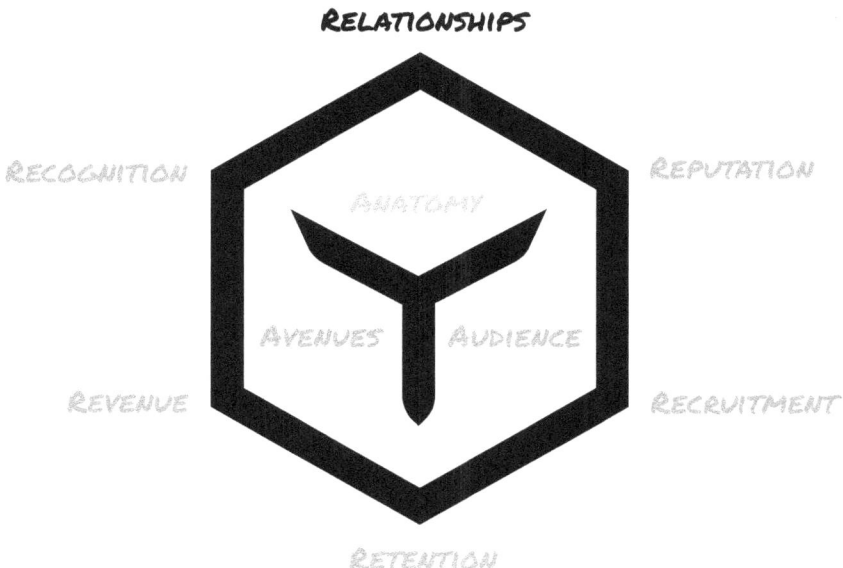

RELATIONSHIPS

RECOGNITION

REPUTATION

ANATOMY

AVENUES AUDIENCE

REVENUE

RECRUITMENT

RETENTION

I've seen it time and time again. Organizations have a false perception of who their most valuable **RELATIONSHIPS** are—or worse yet, mistaken ideas about who their customers are in the first place.

In the early days of HALO, we won an account with one of the largest regional credit unions in the Southwest. As I quizzed them about their audiences and their customer base, they asserted that their customers were incredibly satisfied and they'd collected data to support that belief.

I said, "Great, let's see the numbers and get into it."

You can imagine my shock, then, when I looked through the stack of documents and realized that the data wasn't about their customers. It detailed overall satisfaction trends within the credit union industry.

After a bit of convincing, they agreed to do a three-day focus group with some of their customers and customers of other financial institutions, segmented with different audiences such as business owners, blue-collar and white-collar workers, and so on.

If you've ever been part of a focus group session, you can picture the scene. The attendees were in comfortable seats around a conference room table, freshly stocked with coffee and donuts, while the credit union's CEO, executive team, and I were on the other side of a one-way mirror to observe the proceedings.

As the day went on, I remember watching the furrowed brows and dropping jaws amongst the leadership team as the unvarnished truth was revealed. They believed they had great products and **RELATIONSHIPS**. They came into the sessions confident that they had a well-respected brand in their market.

As we listened to consistent criticisms from their customers, it became clear that wasn't the case. With the exception of a few niche products, there was hardly a strong relationship in the bunch.

They had made a significant push into digital space because that's where they'd seen other financial institutions going. While that was an understandable desire, they hadn't gained the traction they wanted. Part of the issue was that a large population of their target audience was older, and therefore more suitable for marketing with mailers and newspapers. You need to leverage your efforts to the audience where they are!

But we all like happy endings, right? We helped them create a strategy and an advertising campaign, using the data we collected during the focus groups and some additional research, then applying the same tools you're reading about in this book. Through analysis and data building, light bulbs started to go off as they understood who their customers really were—rather than who they thought they wanted.

The strategy required a far more targeted approach than they'd used in the past. Where they previously had marketed to everyone in a particular ZIP Code, we got them to think at a granular level. How could they build a relationship with 18- to 24-year-old males, or 50- to 58-year-old females, or any other specific cohort? What value were those potential customers looking for from the credit union, and what would make them feel valued in a relationship, given those distinct audiences? It wasn't just about building *RELATIONSHIPS* in general, but rather identifying the attributes that could build the right *RELATIONSHIPS*. You need to understand your own company's DNA, and the DNA of the people you want to sell to.

The eventual ad campaign revolved around—you guessed it—relationship building. Instead of trying to compete with other banks, they dialed in on individual customer personas that were a fit for their products and services. They advertised in the venues that would reach the right target audiences with the right messaging, using a blend of print and online. The campaign was a huge hit, and even got an unsolicited mention from the mayor in his annual state of the city address as an example of positive community impact.

More important to the credit union, of course, was how a relationship-based approach impacted their bottom line: A $5 million investment generated nearly $500 million in topline *REVENUE*.

WHAT ARE RELATIONSHIPS?

As we did with **RECOGNITION**, let's step back and define some terms. **RELATIONSHIPS** are connections between people, places, and things. They serve as the cornerstone of every business and act as the main driver of opportunities for **REVENUE** generation in B2B, B2C, and non-profit settings.

I alluded to this in the opening anecdote above, but let's make it crystal clear: The overarching principle to keep in mind is what we call. . .

THE THREE V'S OF HALO

- What *value* is someone looking for from our organization? What value do we provide our customers? **(BENEFIT)**
- What are our like-minded *values*? **(STANDARDS)**
- How can we make them feel *valued* in a relationship with us through our products and services? **(ACTIONS)**

RELATIONSHIPS are built on trust, rapport, and an exchange of value, and they represent a promise a business will fulfill for its connection with another business, a customer, or a nonprofit organization. In terms of the connections between the 6R's, **RELATIONSHIPS** are building on the **RECOGNITION** we discussed in the previous chapter, and they influence **REPUTATION**, which can lead to opportunities for **REVENUE** generation.

At the procedural level, marketing drives marketing-qualified leads (MQL) and the sales team converts the MQL to a sales-qualified lead (SQL) using relationship-building techniques and qualification measures—all with the intention of closing the deal. This process, defined by HALO as the *integrated business cycle* for a business, is often ill-defined or undefined and is often an area with the most opportunity for improvement to support consistent revenue generation and operational efficiency. (More to come on this topic in chapter 8.) In one case, we identified how a client could save $3 million a year in person-hours by improving their integrated business cycle alone.

While business development and sales nurture **RELATIONSHIPS**, however, they're not flying solo. (No more silos, right?) Everyone, from your operations team to frontline client service experts, needs to ensure that the relationship is built.

Businesses typically look to build **RELATIONSHIPS** with two strategic external audiences:

PROSPECTS/CUSTOMERS/CLIENTS. The audiences that can benefit directly from a product or service are often the primary **RELATIONSHIPS** a business would like to build. High-quality **RELATIONSHIPS** with prospects, in which both recognize the exchange of value, are also crucial for creating opportunities for **REVENUE** generation.

PARTNERS. Partners, or those who can refer a product or service offered by a certain business, are **RELATIONSHIPS** that are often equally important. **RELATIONSHIPS** with strategic partners that align with the market or industry of a particular company widen that company's network. High-quality **RELATIONSHIPS** with partners boost brand **RECOGNITION** and improve **REPUTATION**, and expose a company to additional prospects and **REVENUE** opportunities.

RELATIONSHIPS need to be a priority regardless of the size or maturity of your business, and whether you're product or service oriented.

You've probably built a relationship with your preferred car brands, and eventually with your car itself—you want something that reliably takes your family around town or crawls over the tops of off-road boulders, if that's your thing. You have your favorite brands of shoes and clothing, maybe because of the way they make you feel and look, or for how long they last. **RELATIONSHIPS** are the reason why people always go back to Disney World or to Hawaii, or their favorite restaurant or hotel chain, with fond memories building connections.

RELATIONSHIPS are a chemical reaction, and under the right circumstances, it's something your business can control. Not every relationship is right, it takes work to find the right ones. At the same time, it's not something you can just push—in other words, you can't just focus on what you want out of a connection. **RELATIONSHIPS** need to be reciprocal.

Even though the word "relationship" may sound touchy-feely, it's paramount that you are measuring results. Remember, HALO is all about being analytical, not anecdotal (knowing you'll succeed rather than hoping).

If you hang your hat on exceptional customer service, but you don't ask how you're doing or spend the time to identify the three V's of the person or company you're building a relationship with, then you don't know. You're just guessing.

If you spend most of your time focused on what you want, as opposed to building rapport and delivering value, that's not a relationship. It's a one-way street.

If you're waiting for someone to call and give you kudos, or to fire off an email to you when they're dissatisfied, that's not a relationship plan. It's a time bomb waiting to go off.

If you're immediately thinking about how to leverage data or feedback—"How can we use it on our website or emails? How can we turn it into a testimonial to get more people to buy our product?"—that's putting the *REVENUE* cart before the *RELATIONSHIPS* horse.

One final caveat when it comes to measuring: I love sales professionals as much as anyone—they make it all happen. But if your measurement of customer satisfaction includes self-reported testimonials from sales reps on how well they're doing, you're stuck in the anecdotal world. Any salesperson who tells you "My customer loves me and said I'm doing a fantastic job" might be honest or they might be shading the truth.

The only way to know for sure is to harvest the data, including customer testimonials, and to create an action plan from it.

Keep in mind, customers, clients, prospects, partners, and employees wield a lot more power, thanks to social media. Do good, and they'll sing your praises. Do bad, and it will spread like wildfire. The good news is that the digital world also makes it easier to collect and process information about your *RELATIONSHIPS*, but don't fall into the trap of comparing yourself to other businesses or brands that may have initiatives on a larger scale. That's not the point. Keep it simple, then hold yourself accountable.

With HALO, the idea is to meet you where you are right now.

WHAT METRICS SHOULD I USE TO MEASURE RELATIONSHIPS?

For prospects, the following metrics are the most commonly used by HALO clients:

- *Leads (#)*
- *Opportunities (#)*
- *Conversion rate (%)*
- *Pipeline value ($)*
- *Win rate (%)*

Not surprisingly, measuring partner **RELATIONSHIPS** comes down to similar metrics:

- *Leads (#)*
- *Opportunities (#)*
- *Referrals (#)*
- *Conversion rate (%)*
- *Pipeline value ($)*
- *Win rate (%)*

Although it's highly dependent on your type of business, there are numerous routes to measuring the satisfaction of your current customers/clients:

- *Net promoter score (NPS) (#)*
- *Yelp/Google/other online reviews (#,%)*
- *Client/customer satisfaction (%)*

WHERE DO YOU STAND WHEN IT COMES TO RELATIONSHIPS?

EXERCISE #1   **Pain Scale**

You'll recognize this exercise from the previous chapter, and the process is exactly the same. Each member of your team should circle the face that describes their feeling about your company's current state of **RELATIONSHIPS**.

RELATIONSHIPS

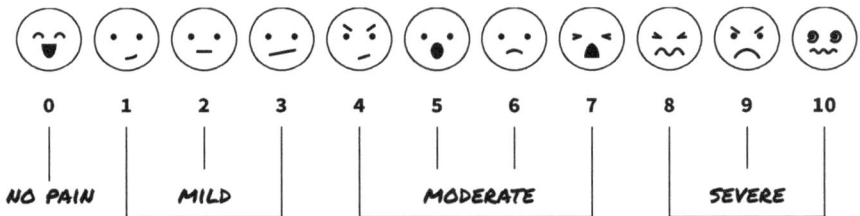

| 0 | 1 | 2 | 3 | 4 | 5 | 6 | 7 | 8 | 9 | 10 |

NO PAIN   MILD   MODERATE   SEVERE

Note: It can be valuable to separate this exercise into prospects, customers, and partners, since the pain scales may be significantly different.

As before, collect the worksheets, total the numbers, average them, and enter the number in the pain scale hexagon matrix on page 179.

If you want to have a further discussion about **RELATIONSHIPS** at this point, I encourage you to do so—particularly if the overall average is six or higher, or if the opinions about pain levels are all over the board.

EXERCISE #2   **Obstacles and Opportunities**

As you may recall, the goal of the second exercise is to connect your 30,000-foot strategic objective with success metrics. Identifying obstacles and opportunities helps identify a clear roadmap for businesses, illuminating potential pitfalls and prospects that directly influence the formulation of strategic plans. This proactive approach aids in focusing resources effectively, enhancing executions, and fostering sustainable growth by navigating obstacles and leveraging opportunities.

During your discussion, you will consider both your current tactics (what are we currently doing to build **RELATIONSHIPS**?) and future strategy (how can increasing relationship quality lead to future revenue-generating opportunities?).

The Obstacles/Opportunities process will help fill in the actions and tactics to link them together. So let's get started.

OBSTACLES

What is standing in the way of building the **RELATIONSHIPS** needed to grow our business? Do we have the right metrics and processes in place to improve our **RELATIONSHIPS**?

List
- Example: Time, Money, Talent, Experience. . .

OPPORTUNITIES

What business development opportunities will help build **RELATIONSHIPS** for our business?

List
- Example: Marketing, Advertising, Networking, Joining Associations. . .

Depending on the results of the exercise, you may want to have a deeper discussion with your HALO group—including an entirely separate session on **RELATIONSHIPS**.

DON'T NEGLECT YOUR EMPLOYEE RELATIONSHIPS

While our immediate focus is on external relationships such as prospects and partners, I want to point out another gap that too many companies have within their relationship matrix: internal relationships. When was the last time you asked your employees if they're satisfied with their relationship with you?

Sure, as an organization, we want our employees to be driving top- and bottom-line revenue. But if that's how they perceive the dynamic, you're taking a quick route to short **RELATIONSHIPS**. If they feel like they offer no value beyond revenue, or that you don't care about them on a personal level, it's only natural that there's an equal and opposite reaction: Your company has no value to them beyond a paycheck. And guess what? At that point, they're going to build weak **RELATIONSHIPS** with your customers, and therefore your customers are going to leave as well. (This also has serious implications when we get to recruiting and retaining employees, and I'll discuss those topics at greater length when I get to those chapters.)

It's not uncommon for businesses to resist wanting to solicit employee feedback, because they fear what their answers are going to be. I hate to break it to you, but ignorance is not bliss. In addition, avoid the temptation to respond only to **RELATIONSHIPS** that are on the poles of super happy or super unhappy—dedicate resources to reaching the middle and moving them toward the 10 on the happiness scale. If you've read this deep into this book to try to improve your company or to improve your division, clearly you're committed enough to take this seriously.

For companies that want to measure internal satisfaction, there are a number of different options. My go-to recommendation is a software called Officevibe. It automates the ability to send out a short anonymous survey every week. The questions are fun and constantly changing, while they generate a wealth of data that allows you to track trends in happiness, health, and wellness.

RELATIONSHIPS IN THE REAL WORLD. . . DONE RIGHT

When I think about **RELATIONSHIPS** that exemplify the HALO approach, I always turn to a few specific examples. The first is the online shoe store Zappos. The number-one metric they track is client satisfaction and relationships. Theoretically, they're just selling shoes, right? But to them, everything revolves around customer service, not just the number of transactions and how much revenue they were generating. That's the reason for their no-questions-asked return policy, price matching with competitors, 24/7 customer service availability, and Zappos for Good donation program. They understand that, if they have a good relationship, their customer is going to feel valued—and they aren't going to go someplace else for footwear.

Patagonia is built to create **RELATIONSHIPS** on a variety of levels. Not only do they manufacture the best products in the outdoors industry, they value our collective relationship with the Earth, donating countless millions of dollars to environmental conservation. Patagonia's late founder, Yvon Chouinard, also got the internal **RELATIONSHIPS** right. One legendary story was that he was on his annual wilderness sabbatical when a fire occurred at the factory. When the staff contacted him to find out what to do, his response was simple: He told them he trusted them to solve the problem. There's no better example of the relationship that a CEO or owner can—and should—have with their people. He understood better than anyone how vital **RELATIONSHIPS** are.

In our household, my wife is the handy one. Sure, we might be able to get the supplies for a DIY project cheaper at Home Depot or Lowe's. But when we go to Ace Hardware, we actually get solutions. If there's some oddball screw we need, they'll be able to find it. If it's a more complex repair, they'll automatically ask if we have the right tools at home or the two or three adjacent parts that go with it. Their secret sauce is in staffing subject matter experts who will help you get the job done, and keep you coming back.

Although it's not the best coffee in the world, my preference is Starbucks because I have a relationship with the brand. Wherever I am, in any city or state on every continent, I can walk into a Starbucks and I'll know exactly what I'm going to get. Starbucks invests in our relationship through their loyalty program, and by creating comfortable environments that, as a business owner, I can use to work no matter where I am.

On a more local level, I think about our annual family trip to New Hampshire, in a tiny town with two stop lights and two pizza joints. The food is basically the same in both places, but we always go to Village Pizza. The owner and the staff have far superior customer service, so they win our family vote every time. They understand that business is personal, and they care about the people coming in.

Airlines are a mixed bag. Whether it's United, American, or Southwest, I can't name an airline that does a great job with **RELATIONSHIPS** in the current environment. They're desperate to drive **REVENUE** and profitability, full stop. But then you look at the trends in airports themselves, and it gives me a glimmer of hope. My hometown airport, Phoenix Sky Harbor International, has undergone an amazing transformation in recent years, with tons of local restaurants having locations in the terminals. I've seen the trend elsewhere across the country, moving away from chains and towards introducing passengers to the culture of a city—encouraging a relationship and further exploration.

Finally, I love to talk about Joseph Samuel Girard, a car salesman who sold more than 13,000 cars at a Chevrolet dealership between 1963 and 1978—and in his peak year, outsold 90% of the dealerships in North America.[9] His investment in cultivating relationships was beyond belief, mailing out personalized cards to thousands of customers every year. He'd remember where you worked, your kids' names, and a whole host of other information that most people in the car sales world would forget the moment you walked out the door. But beyond that, he made his customers feel valued. He wasn't trying to sell the most expensive car, but to get you something that fit so that you'd have a positive relationship with the vehicle, too. In an industry with a terrible reputation, he proved the power of building a relationship for life.

"Is This the Right Relationship for Us?"

That last piece, customer lifetime value, is what **RELATIONSHIPS** are all about. If you have good **RELATIONSHIPS** and serve people appropriately, it leads to sustainable **REVENUE**. For many businesses, in fact, **RELATIONSHIPS** are the main driver for **REVENUE** both internally and externally.

When you get down to it, **RELATIONSHIPS** are the point of life. They're the core of what makes us human.

People don't want to be sold to—they want mutually beneficial **RELATIONSHIPS** based on the three V's.

At the same time, you're not just cultivating **RELATIONSHIPS** for the sake of it. **RELATIONSHIPS** are a building block for your future vision of success, which means always asking "Is this the right relationship for us?" For external **RELATIONSHIPS**, that means looking beyond the short-term **REVENUE** generation aspects and ensuring that a client or partner is the correct fit over the longer haul. For internal **RELATIONSHIPS**, it applies to **RECRUITMENT** and **RETENTION**, making sure

---

9   "How the Greatest Salesman of All Time Sold 13,001 Cars in His Career," https://bettermarketing.pub/how-the-greatest-salesman-of-all-time-sold-13-001-cars-in-his-career-d60f15b17ff

you have the right people in the right seats. And, of course, how you develop **RELATIONSHIPS** will determine your success in the 6R that's coming up when you turn to the next chapter: **REPUTATION**.

To download a fillable PDF version of the exercises
in this chapter, visit *haloforall.com/hrh*

Six Key Takeaways

1. **REVENUE** happens when you focus on the three V's of HALO: What value is someone looking for from us? What are our like-minded values? How will they feel valued in a relationship with us through our products and services?

2. High-quality **RELATIONSHIPS** with prospects, in which both recognize the exchange of value, are crucial for creating opportunities for **REVENUE** generation.

3. High-quality **RELATIONSHIPS** with partners boost brand **RECOGNITION** and improve Reputation, which also offers **REVENUE** opportunities.

4. Avoid the temptation to respond only to **RELATIONSHIPS** that are on the poles of super happy or super unhappy—dedicate resources to reaching the middle and moving them toward the 10 on the happiness scale.

5. While business development and sales play the key role, everyone in the organization has relationship responsibilities.

6. Don't compare yourself to other businesses or brands with more sophisticated programs. Keep it simple, then hold yourself accountable.

"It takes 20 years to build a reputation and five minutes to ruin it. If you think about that, you'll do things differently."

—Warren Buffett

CHAPTER 6

REPUTATION:

BUILDING TRUST THROUGH YOUR OPERATIONS

Achieving operational excellence by embodying your core values in every interaction and business decision.

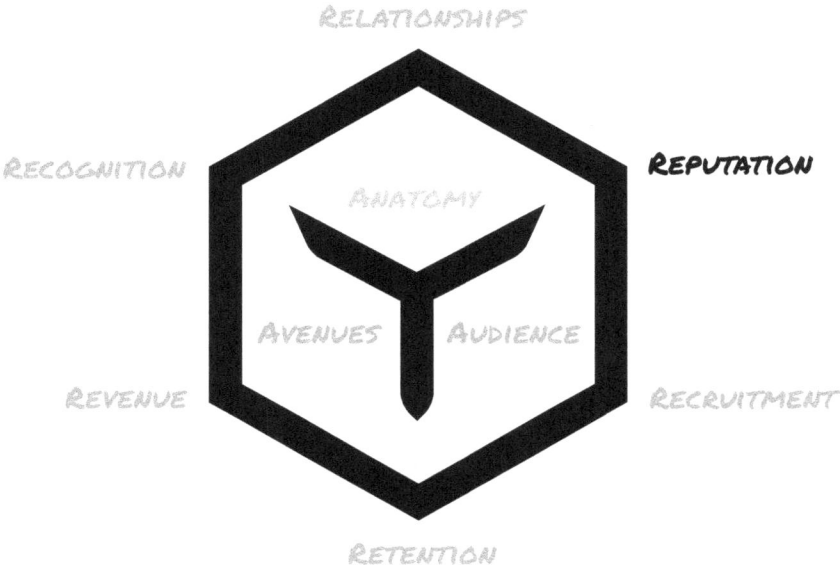

RELATIONSHIPS

RECOGNITION

REPUTATION

ANATOMY

AVENUES   AUDIENCE

REVENUE   RECRUITMENT

RETENTION

At the end of the previous chapter, I listed some of my favorite examples of companies that excel at **RELATIONSHIPS**. Now let's flip it around and look at some **REPUTATION** disasters in recent years, serving as an object lesson in what *not* to do.

Volkswagen/Audi's Dieselgate. In 2015, it was discovered that Volkswagen and Audi had intentionally programmed their TDI turbodiesel engines to evade emissions controls. In simple terms, the cars' software had been programmed to artificially lower emissions when being tested—then, back on the road, they produced about 40 times as much nitrogen oxide. About 11 million vehicles built from 2009 through 2015 were affected, nearly half a million US owners were offered a buyback, and the total costs of penalties, fines, and buybacks ran upwards of $35 billion. Those weren't the only costs, however, because the **REPUTATION** damage is still echoing. Volkswagen/Audi hurt their revenues so much that they had to kill projects. A company that once prided itself on quality engineering now swapped in cheaper plastic parts that used to be metal. Those are the bigger implications, because it points to abandoning their operational standards and principles. The initial decision to cheat has affected everything about their brand and **RELATIONSHIPS** with partners and customers.

Wells Fargo Cross-Selling Scandal. In 2016, this was a classic case of senior leadership prioritizing revenue above all else—and breaking laws in the process. In order to hit quotas, employees were encouraged to cross-sell: creating millions of fake checking and savings accounts for the bank's customers, and even ordering credit cards using their own personal information so the clients wouldn't know. In addition to hundreds of millions of dollars in fines, there were billions in civil and criminal suits, more than 5,000 employees were fired, and two CEOs were canned as well. It's impossible to even calculate the **REPUTATION** damage, but let's just say it's never good when your CEO is hauled in front of the US Senate Banking Committee to explain their actions.

Southwest Airlines Scheduling Crisis. A historic winter storm and cold snap that started on December 21, 2022, caused problems and flight cancellations throughout the airline industry during one of the busiest travel periods of the year. While carriers such as American and Delta soon got back on schedule, the situation at Southwest only got worse—with about 15,000 cancellations in an eight-day period and 60% of their flights canceled between December 26 to 28. It became clear that it wasn't just about snow and freezing temperatures; the airline's antiquated operations system had been overwhelmed, including the ability to manage flight crews and customer service reps. It wasn't even a surprise; Southwest was aware their systems were a ticking time bomb, since they'd had smaller but similar issues in previous years. Although the airline plans to spend $1.3 billion to upgrade their technology, that's not a cure for a busted **REPUTATION**. I can guarantee that many of the people who got stranded for days, lost luggage, or had to make a 12-hour rental car drive with strangers aren't going to be flying Southwest again anytime soon.

With those horror shows fresh in your mind, I'll point to the contrast with a few companies who stand by their anatomy, live by their core values, take care of their customers, and don't skimp just to drive more revenue. I've extolled the virtues of Zappos and Patagonia previously, so think about examples like:

- *REI, which isn't open on Black Friday—in other words, the **REPUTATION** of caring for their people is more important to them than the revenue they'd get on the biggest shopping day of the year. And even for their customers, the message is "You have the day off—please enjoy the great outdoors and don't come shopping at our place! We'll be here when you get back from your adventure."*

- *Costco, which showed leadership through the Covid pandemic, protecting their employees and customers, but also has one of the most amazing return policies in the retail world. I could cart in a broken TV that I bought from them five years ago, way past warranty expiration, and they would still take it back. That's part of the promise that they've made to their members.*

- *United Airlines, which is trying to change not only their corporate **REPUTATION**, but the reputation for the entire airline industry. United recently revamped their policy so passengers can change flights without incurring a change fee for most types of fares. It's going to take a lot to change the airline industry's image of being* *money-hungry nickel-and-dimers, of course, but it will be a step in the right direction if other airlines follow suit.*

- *In-N-Out Burger, which used to be a California-only joint but now turns into a phenomenon wherever they expand, thanks to a **REPUTATION** for quality, fresh food, and pleasant service. I lived in Tucson when they got their first location there, and for months there was a two-hour wait to get a hamburger and French fries. They had no existing market in Arizona's second-largest city, but their **REPUTATION** preceded itself.*

To improve your **REPUTATION**, you need to run your business more like those latter examples than the former. When companies deliver on their promise, their **REPUTATION** takes flight. Let's talk about how you can create a system to accomplish that.

WHAT IS REPUTATION?

REPUTATION is how outsiders view your products, services, brand, and leadership.

Perception, as they say, is reality: A company's **REPUTATION** is everything in the eyes of the prospect. Yet, I'd argue that it's something that organizations don't spend enough time thinking about, and they don't always make the direct connection to their operations that is needed. Part of that is a lack of understanding about how **REPUTATION** is built and its cascade of influence.

REPUTATION is a hub with a lot of spokes. How your business is recognized in the marketplace, particularly with new audiences and new markets. The types of **RELATIONSHIPS** you have with partners and clients. How hard it is to recruit new employees and retain top performers. Add it all up, and it's an essential part of how your revenues are generated and maintained.

Consider a few cold, hard facts:

- *A dissatisfied customer will tell between 9 and 15 people about their experience.[10] (Of course, based on the current environment, an online influencer could also broadcast to tens or hundreds of thousands of people in a split second.)*

- *It can take more than three years for a business to recover from reputational damage, and in some cases, much, much longer—if ever.*

- *It's estimated that 93% of consumers read online reviews for local businesses before making a decision. Depending on what industry you're in, that number could be much higher.[11]*

- *The difference between four stars and five stars can be 18% in revenue. Yes, that's for a one-star difference.*

We're all familiar with **REPUTATION** in the form of Google and Amazon reviews, Yelp, Glassdoor, and a million other ways that customers and employees weigh in on how we're doing. But that's the end effect of your **REPUTATION** building and management efforts, not the start. Too few companies consider their responsibility and accountability in the process: how they play a pivotal role in building and delivering that perception for the person who's going to review them or comment on their **REPUTATION**.

It's easy to put it off with "Oh, well. My **REPUTATION** is based on what somebody else thinks about my product/service/me."

Or I've had people say, "Rob, I'm a small company. I'm not really going to worry about **REPUTATION** right now."

But I'm telling you, I've seen **REPUTATION** crashes happen to companies of all sizes, and it's not pretty.

---

10   White House Office of Consumer Affairs
11   This statistic and the following statistic are from https://www.qualtrics.com/blog/online-review-stats, which includes additional details about the value of positive reviews and the cost of negative reviews.

REPUTATION revolves around your operations—how you deliver a consistently excellent experience—and enforcing the core values, standards, and principles that are vital to you as an executive or entrepreneur. Put simply, a positive **REPUTATION** can translate to more customers, better employees, and greater profitability—a must in any business endeavor. Not only does a good **REPUTATION** increase the number of customers your business attracts, but it can also increase the quality of those customers.

I want you to correlate **REPUTATION** with operations, but the fact is that every department in your company has a role to play in each of the 6R's. After all, HALO is about breaking down silos. **REPUTATION**, however, is often something in which the various operational functions are more critical than they realize. Every company you can name has a marketing team, sales team, finance team, HR team, and so on. But it's uncommon for me to stumble across a **REPUTATION** team, or a group that serves such a function.

REPUTATION is built through all operations of a business, including its products, services, and business units associated with operations, such as but not limited to:

- *Marketing*
- *Sales/Business Development*
- *Human Resources*
- *I.T.*
- *Accounting/Finance*
- *Manufacturing*
- *Engineering*
- *Leadership/Executive Team/Managers*
- *Customer Service*

Businesses build their **REPUTATION** with every interaction, through prospects and customers engaging with its products, services, and employees. It's through this experience that beliefs and opinions are formed and shared. Brands also build their **REPUTATION** by the company they keep, which is why strategic partnerships with philosophical or market alignment are vital.

WHAT METRICS SHOULD I USE TO MEASURE REPUTATION?

Businesses have the best chance of building their **REPUTATION** by looking for ways to improve the value of their products and services, and focusing on key core values that can be tracked, measured, and communicated to ensure a consistent customer experience. The hard part about this is that you can't just pull a KPI off the shelf to influence your **REPUTATION**—you really have to tack it to your company's anatomy.

Some of the metrics commonly used by HALO clients include:

- *Core values metrics (#,%)*
- *Operating metrics (#,%)*
- *Customer satisfaction scores (%)*
- *Net promoter score (#)*
- *Online reviews (#)*
- *Testimonials (#)*
- *Referrals (#)*

WHERE DO YOU STAND WHEN IT COMES TO REPUTATION?

EXERCISE #1   Pain Scale

You know the drill by now. Ask your team to discuss the definition of **REPUTATION**, and then have each participant circle the face that describes their feeling about your company's current state.

REPUTATION

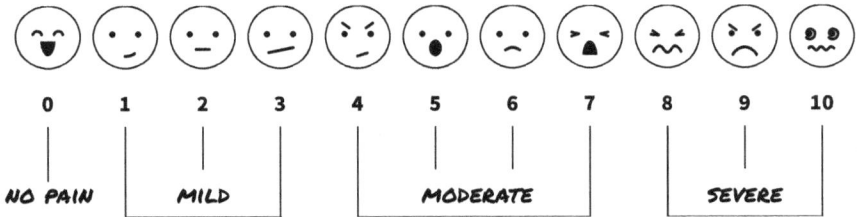

0	1	2	3	4	5	6	7	8	9	10

NO PAIN   MILD   MODERATE   SEVERE

Note: This is definitely an exercise that should be split into prospects, customers, partners, and employees, since the pain scales may be significantly different.

As you've done for the past several R's, collect the worksheets, total the numbers, average them, and enter the number in the pain scale hexagon matrix on page 179.

You can tell how strongly I believe in the importance of **REPUTATION**. If the overall pain-scale average is six or higher, or if the opinions are divergent, I encourage conducting a deeper discussion with your team.

EXERCISE #2   **Obstacles and Opportunities**

Once again, we need to connect your 30,000-foot strategic objective with success metrics. Identifying obstacles and opportunities helps identify a clear roadmap for businesses, illuminating potential pitfalls and prospects that directly influence the formulation of strategic plans. This proactive approach aids in focusing resources effectively, enhancing execution, and fostering sustainable growth by navigating obstacles and leveraging opportunities.

During your discussion, please consider both your current tactics (what are we currently doing to build **REPUTATION**?) and future strategy (how can increasing our **REPUTATION** quality lead to future **REVENUE**-generating opportunities?).

The Obstacles/Opportunities process is designed to link your actions and tactics together. Let's go.

OBSTACLES

What is standing in the way of building the **REPUTATION** needed to grow our business? Do we have the right metrics and processes in place to improve our **REPUTATION**?

List
- *Example: Time, Money, Talent, Experience...*

OPPORTUNITIES

What operational opportunities will help build **REPUTATION** for our business?

List
- *Example: Improving Culture, Better Products/Services, Improved Logisitics...*

Depending on the departments you choose to include, this can be a more extensive exercise than with some of the other R's. Consider taking a deeper dive with your HALO group—including an entirely separate session on **REPUTATION** within each of the individual groups.

YOU'RE A LEADER. ACT LIKE IT

In one of our recent HALO forums, one of the participants—the CEO of a midsize company—asked an interesting question: "How do I separate my personal DNA from the brand's DNA?" My answer was that you don't necessarily want to do that. Instead, as a leader, you want to find the commonality. As the executive or entrepreneur, the business is an extension of you, and your own DNA needs to be part of that.

As a result, it's a good time for you and your leadership team to think about your own core values. How are those going to help you build your business? How will they be reflected in your interactions with clients, customers, prospects, partners, and employees?

I say that because, among all those departments listed in the exercise above, the most important people to building the **REPUTATION** are the executive leadership—and their actions are highly leveraged to be positive or negative. Leadership sets the tone for **REPUTATION**. We can see that in the largely positive influence of Patagonia's Yvon Chouinard or Nike's Phil Knight, or in the mixed bag that is Elon Musk at Tesla, SpaceX, and the X social media platform.

I've seen too many companies that take the Michael Scott approach to **REPUTATION**, which is to say constantly chasing after every "opportunity" that comes their way—which leads to erratic behavior, lack of organization, and the tendency to prioritize entertainment over work. It's fun to watch on TV, but much less fun to live through in a work environment. Without a clear focus on what your company wants its **REPUTATION** to be, you'll spend more time parkouring off the walls of your building than building and delivering quality products and services.

If you say you want a **REPUTATION** for the best service or product in your industry, that needs to be weaved through everything you do on the operations side, not just winning the work—because your employees know when you are full of it. Don't forget, you have competition who's making similar claims about their own quality, and they have a **REPUTATION** of their own. You have to continue to prove yourself within the market of your customers' options, not to mention the options available to prospects and partners.

Operational excellence is about embodying your core values in every single interaction and business decision that you make—and reinforcing that throughout your organization. That includes the people you hire, the products you build, the services that you promise, and the experience that customers have over the course of their relationship with you.

REPUTATION matters because your core values matter. I won't get into the gory details, but I had an experience with a healthcare provider that claimed customer success was one of their core values. It was a disaster, putting one of my loved ones on the brink of death based on massive errors. Yet nobody ever captured our feedback. It never went into a metric that got discussed outside the room, let alone at the corporate level.

You're also building your **REPUTATION** by the company that you keep, including strategic partners with philosophical or market alignment. At the same time, it's not my job to try to change my partners. It's my job to control what I can control, and if **REPUTATION** is important to me, then I'm going to be careful about the partners that I build **RELATIONSHIPS** with. When a partner, vendor, or other relationship doesn't fit, or if you see questionable behaviors that could put you at risk, you have to have the courage and discipline to say "This isn't good for us."

Whether you're a small company or a huge one, whether you're in startup mode or hunting for acquisitions and mergers, **REPUTATION** comes down to operational discipline. That's how your **REPUTATION** is built—and it starts from the top.

THE GAME HAS CHANGED. . . AND YOUR APPROACH MUST TOO

Think about your experiences on Amazon when buying a product you haven't used before, or opening Yelp for a restaurant recommendation for date night. When you have countless options, you're probably going to deviate towards the highest reviews—even if it's the difference between 4.2 stars and 4.3 stars. We've been trained to look for that in our decision making. Maybe we'll look at the reviews, with the knowledge that some of the good ones and bad ones might be paid, and we don't have a relationship with someone who can vouch for the validity.

Before the digital disruption of the early 2000s, whatever you marketed and advertised about your company was how you built your **REPUTATION**. There was no social media, no crowdsourcing of opinions, no mobs of raving fans or vicious haters. Your **REPUTATION** was basically what you said it was and what people said about you.

REPUTATION equals trust and comfort, but no one will just take your word for it. If you're building your **REPUTATION** through your operations, based on your products and services, then you will be nurturing **RELATIONSHIPS** with people who will both speak highly of you and be loyal customers. When entering a new market, however, you don't have the luxury of tons of **RECOGNITION** or **RELATIONSHIPS**. People are hesitant to try the new thing. Any trust and comfort—and confidence that you can solve their pain point—will rely on the aggregate **REPUTATION** you've built through other sources to help someone make their decision.

If you're in an established market, the primary way to improve your **REPUTATION** is to get your current customer base to speak highly about you because you service them well. Fail at that, and you're not going to get referrals and you're not going to grow. When you're underperforming, you can't push the stone uphill.

Whatever widget or service that you're selling, people are going to do more due diligence at higher price points. It's worth noting that the stakes are par- ticularly high if your business revolves around immediate or emergency needs, for example plumbing or roofing. Those companies have to spend significant effort on building **REPUTATION**, because the decision-making process has a short window: my kitchen sink is clogged or the roof is leaking. The vast majority of those prospects—I'd bet over 95%—will make an immediate decision based on **REPUTATION** and reviews. It's also why companies like that need to have their operations dialed in: The customer is already in a situation that is urgent and possibly expensive, and they need to feel confident the job will be done right.

Focus on What You Can Control, Not Whack-a-Mole

People have no problem airing out what they don't like about something. Restaurant, car, pair of shoes, appliances, doctor's office, law practice, real estate agent, plumber, or house painter, it doesn't matter. Give people the chance to rant about what they don't like, they'll do it till they're blue in the face. It's a fine line between responding to negative comments—trying to right wrongs, bridge gaps, and build trust—versus wasting your time screaming into the abyss.

A key piece of HALO in relation to **REPUTATION** is accepting that you're not going to be able to control everything. You're not going to be able to shut out everyone who doesn't fully align with your three V's. What you're trying to do is give yourself parameters to make decisions that are in the best interest of your business and yourself.

I had a sports medicine client that wrestled terribly with this. Their client base included several national professional sports teams, but I'll never forget a conversation I had with one of their doctors. He was up in arms, because sports management and physical therapists end up dealing with a lot of drug seekers—people who are just looking for a prescription for pain medications, not to solve a problem. And maybe it's not a surprise, but they're the first people to go online and torch you in a review.

"Rob," he said. "I need to stop these people, because they're dragging us down. I want to address every single one of them."

My response was simple. "That's not a good use of your time," I said. "It's a game of whack-a-mole. Even if you manage to take one down, there's going to be 10 more."

Instead of getting out the hammer, he approached the situation strategically. The first step was to do a better job of screening and identifying the green, yellow, and red lights of the types of customer they were trying to attract. But the second, more important part was to tap into the thousands of professional athletes and other customers who'd had a good experience with his practice. They hadn't been diligent about asking for positive reviews—which was really the only thing they could control. Ultimately, they were able to flood out the bad reviews with good ones, and their **REPUTATION** responded accordingly.

It can even be as simple as making it easy for customers to cancel. If you're among the millions of people who've cut the cable cord, you know the hassle your provider puts you through—and we all know how poor cable company reputations are. Gyms are notorious for the same strategy, with many of them requiring you to drive to their facility just to cancel. That's a terrific way of cementing in my head that you want to make it as difficult as possible to have a relationship with you. I want the lifting to be hard, I don't want the relationship to be hard.

By comparison, I think about my experience with Ka'Chava, a company that produces a line of tasty organic meal replacement shakes. I'd been subscribed to their service for a while, but one day I felt kind of burned out on them and decided to turn it off. Six months later, I woke up and saw a charge for $150, because the subscription automatically turned on.

I wasn't happy. But I jumped on their website chat at 7 a.m., and had the situation resolved and my money refunded in under two minutes. Here's the key: They couldn't control how upset I was going to be, but they could control how they interacted—and it was exceptional. For that reason alone, I will go back to their service again at some point, because they turned a negative experience into a positive.

There's nothing wrong with saying "Is there anything that I can do to keep you as a customer?" but it's shortsighted to fight someone if they have made their position clear.

NAVIGATING THE GENERATIONAL FACTOR

Within your company, your approach needs to take generational differences into consideration. It's a significant challenge for entrepreneurs and executives—or anyone else in a position of power—who've been brought up in an entirely different culture to meet the needs of the up-and-comers in their organization. Work-life balance and mental health days weren't a thing when many of us were climbing the corporate ladder, let alone the concept of work from home, four-hour workdays, or showing up to meetings 15 minutes late. At the risk of sounding older than I am, back in the day, you'd get fired in 20 seconds for a lot of behaviors that are tolerated now.

On the flip side of that, Mr. Buffett's five-minutes-to-a-ruined-reputation cited at the top of the chapter can now occur in 10 seconds in a viral video. Like it or not, there's a line of people waiting for you to screw up—and as sad as it sounds, they care more about trending on TikTok than they do about their career.

That's why you need to find a way to align yourself and your company, and everyone who has a relationship inside and out. Organizations need to think more holistically, because one false step can unravel your **REPUTATION** in a way that damages the other five R's in a hurry. Conversely, one awesome step and your positive **REPUTATION** is amplified to millions of new customers! You have to break down the walls that you typically put up to prevent people from seeing how the sausage is made. For anyone who wants to be an entrepreneur or executive, these are the new rules of engagement.

Once again, I'm going to point to the three V's as your touchstone when it comes to employees and **REPUTATION** management:

- *What is their value to me? What is our value to them? (Benefit)*

- *What are our like-minded values? (Standards)*

- *How do I make them feel valued? (Actions)*

The pendulum has swung, but that doesn't mean you need to get hit in the private parts with it.

PUSHING THROUGH THE DISCOMFORT

Part of my own **REPUTATION** as a consultant is being the guy who's always asking "Why?" I'm proud of that, because the results that individuals will get—even when I'm gone—will significantly outweigh their discomfort with me in the moment. Usually the people I've rubbed the wrong way are the ones hiding in plain sight, lacking accountability, deflecting, and deferring. They're the ones who don't want to be exposed, who prefer a safe, fixed mindset rather than tackling the hard tasks of growth.

But you know what? At the end of one of those incredibly direct, difficult conversations, I will literally say "I love you." More often than not, I'll hear it back.

There is a difference between being right and being necessary. I don't aim to always be right—but my actions and tactics are necessary to overcome obstacles and seize opportunities with and for clients.

So if you're feeling like you've been inattentive to your **REPUTATION** issues, I want that to fuel your fire. I'm not saying your baby is ugly because I don't like your baby; I'm trying to be honest with you. And in the interest of full disclosure, I will admit to failures of **REPUTATION** in my own business life.

If I went through my old client list at the ad agency, I would find plenty of people who would give me glowing reviews. Being honest with myself, however, we didn't have as many referrals or advocates as we could have, because I didn't ask. There are also individuals who had a less-than-stellar experience, whether it was a matter of overpromising and underdelivering, or guiding them towards a solution they weren't ready for. In the advertising world, you're only as good as the results of your last campaign. I own that.

In the same way, I want you to be honest with yourself and your team about why your **REPUTATION** may be falling short—and it's not just because people don't know how great you are. How did you participate? Why did things not go according to plan?

I'm pushing you because that's part of making **REPUTATION** a priority. Not to get all mushy about it, but it's coming from a place of love.

To download a fillable PDF version of the exercises
in this chapter, visit *haloforall.com/hrh*

Six Key Takeaways

1. Revenue happens when your organization embodies its core values in every interaction and business decision.

2. Leadership sets the tone for **REPUTATION**.

3. Your ability to maintain and build **REPUTATION** is reinforced through operational excellence, including how you deliver products, services and the customer experience.

4. The end goal of your **REPUTATION** strategy is to position your business as reliable and trustworthy.

5. A dissatisfied customer will tell between 9-15 people about their experience, and it can take more than three years for a business to recover from reputational damage.

6. Although Warren Buffett said that it takes just five minutes to ruin your **REPUTATION**, a viral video can do the job in 10 seconds.

"You don't build business, you build people and then people build the business."

— Zig Ziglar

CHAPTER 7

RECRUITMENT:
HIRING IS EASY,
RECRUITING IS HARD

Identifying and attracting talent that's the right match
for your company's anatomy—and future success.

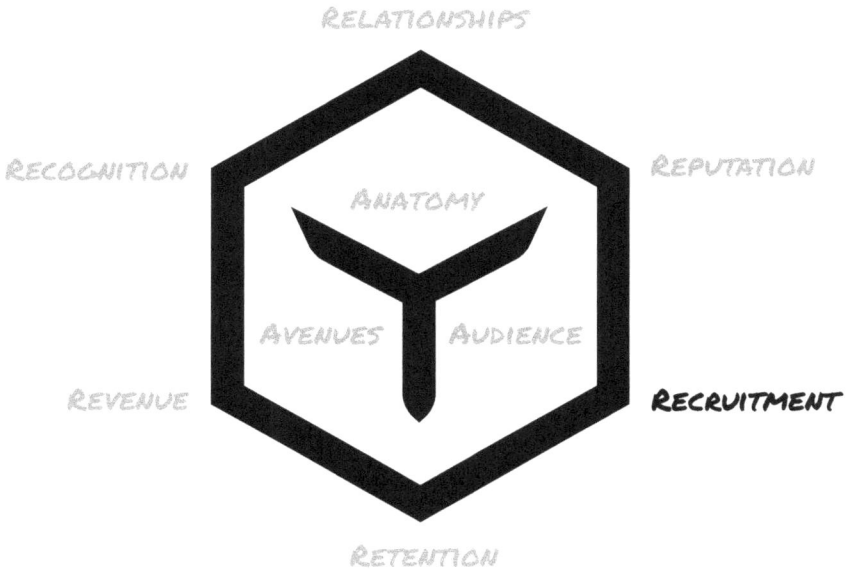

RELATIONSHIPS

RECOGNITION

REPUTATION

ANATOMY

AVENUES   AUDIENCE

REVENUE   **RECRUITMENT**

RETENTION

Finding and securing talent creates a situation with a million variables that can go sideways. You might get lucky and get the right person for the right position, or who can be trained to be that high performer you need. You can hire the right person for the wrong seat, or someone who'd be wrong for your company no matter where their butt spent the time from 9 to 5.

It's easy for an entrepreneur or executive to delay taking action until the pain becomes extreme. Psychologically, that's called *choosing to be confused*—because you don't want to make the hard decision. You're going to give an underperformer another chance and not going to fire them immediately, while the voice inside your head is nagging at you. *Maybe they'll clue into the fact that they stink at their job and get miserable enough to quit, right? Ugh, I'm going to have to post the job again, and maybe spend money on a headhunter. Then we'll need someone to train them till they're up to speed. I can't believe I have to start another relationship from scratch.*

I get it. I don't enjoy dealing with personnel problems either. But in order to surround myself with capable people for my future success, a **RECRUITMENT** strategy is part of the responsibility. You need to avoid the problems in the first place.

WHAT IS RECRUITMENT?

RECRUITMENT is the process of finding the right person to do a specific job for an organization. Notice the word *right*. In order to support the level of quality and service your company needs, the process of finding and hiring people requires intention, and clarity about the roles and positions required to support your future state. Done correctly, that will build your **REPUTATION**. In addition, hiring the right people improves **RETENTION**, which offers a cost savings to a company—since turnover is a costly exercise that ultimately negatively impacts **REVENUE**.

In most cases, **RECRUITMENT** efforts are managed by human resources or talent acquisition departments, and in some cases outside consultants. It's common for marketing to assist with **RECRUITMENT** efforts through paid and organic campaigns to drive **RECOGNITION** about career opportunities as a way to uncover candidate leads.

What's at Stake in Recruitment?

- *Replacing an employee can cost up to 213% of the salary for a highly trained position.*

- *46% of newly hired employees will fail within 18 months, while only 19% will achieve success. Ineffective Recruitment processes can lead to hiring candidates who underperform or are not a good fit for the role.*

- *88% of employers said that a quality hire for them meant a good cultural fit. However, 95% of businesses admitted to recruiting the wrong people each year, indicating ineffective recruiting processes when it came to assessing cultural fit.[12]*

12 https://hiring.monster.com/resources/blog/
    monster-poll-micromanagement-is-the-biggest-workplace-red-flag

The quality of your hires is going to directly impact your ability to drive more **REVENUE**, top-line and bottom-line earnings. A rock-star marketing director will cultivate more and better **RELATIONSHIPS** and increase your **RECOGNITION**. A top-tier salesperson will develop those **RELATIONSHIPS** and convert them into sales. A high-quality operations leader will create a virtuous circle by improving the systems, nailing the metrics on product quality and service quality, and allowing you to run more efficiently and effectively. All of those pieces contribute to **REVENUE**. Conversely, if you fill any of those positions with someone who's doing a poor job, it's going to undermine your **REPUTATION**, **RELATIONSHIPS**, **REVENUE**, and profitability—while creating misery for you and your team.

While **RECRUITMENT** is almost always a priority, there are times when it's most critical. Entering a new market comes with higher risk of failure because you have little or no **RECOGNITION**, **RELATIONSHIPS**, or **REPUTATION**. That puts a premium on recruiting individuals who have the capabilities and the qualities needed to help drive those main R's. How you accomplish that is highly situation dependent, of course. Making community connections, such as tapping into local universities and associations, can be a valuable first step.

Launching a new product or service means recruiting talent from outside your organization—and being extra clear about the team you're assembling. What are the personal qualities and skills of a leader for that situation, given the riskiness of a launch? What are the attributes of the team members, and what are the metrics of success?

For startups and smaller businesses, the stakes are particularly high—more important than for an enterprise business, I'd argue. Since each employee is a larger percentage of your operation and everyone is working more closely—and possibly cross-functionally—there's less margin for a hiring error. It's ironic that the businesses who could benefit most from a savvy **RECRUITMENT** process are often moving so fast they don't have the time to spend thinking about it.

For good or ill, job seekers have more information than ever about you as an employer, through venues such as Glassdoor, ZipRecruiter, or Indeed employee reviews. You may want to choose them, but you also need to get them to choose you.

WHAT METRICS SHOULD I USE TO MEASURE RECRUITMENT?

Consider this a list of items to choose from—I don't recommend trying to implement all of them simultaneously. What's meaningful for your business? What are the most important factors for your company's future success? I've seen a few HALO companies start off by trying to measure too much, measuring the wrong things, or discovering that they needed a metric for something new. It's all part of the natural progression and transition required by change. Hard, messy, then beautiful, right?

RECRUITMENT metrics can also serve as an early warning signal for problems. For example, you listed a job hoping for a minimum of six candidates and it's been up for 90 days with just two applicants. The issue could be the channels the listing was published in, the quality of the writing, the salary, or any number of little things. Failing to hit your average metric alerts you to the issue and gives you a starting point for investigation.

TALENT RECRUITMENT

- *Candidate net promoter score (#)*
- *First-year attrition (#,%)*
- *Fill rate (#,%)*
- *Candidates per hire (#)*
- *Cost of hire ($)*
- *Time to hire (#)*
- *Offer acceptance rate (#,%)*
- *Quality of hire (%)*

WHERE DO YOU STAND WHEN IT COMES TO RECRUITMENT?

EXERCISE #1   ## Pain Scale

It's that time again. Ask your team to discuss the definition of **RECRUITMENT**, and then have each participant circle the face that describes their feeling about your company's current state.

RECRUITMENT

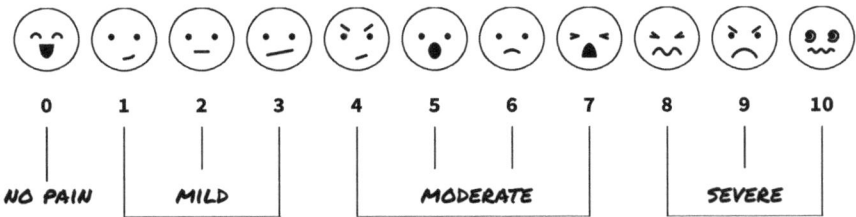

| 0 | 1 | 2 | 3 | 4 | 5 | 6 | 7 | 8 | 9 | 10 |

NO PAIN   MILD   MODERATE   SEVERE

With that done, collect the worksheets, total the numbers, average them, and enter the number in the pain scale hexagon matrix on page 179.

As with the previous R's, If the overall pain-scale average is six or higher, or if the opinions are divergent, I encourage conducting a deeper discussion with your team.

EXERCISE #2   ## Obstacles and Opportunities

During your discussion, please consider both your current tactics (what are we currently doing to improve **RECRUITMENT**?) and future strategy (how can boosting our **RECRUITMENT** results lead to future **REVENUE**-generating opportunities?).

The Obstacles/Opportunities process is designed to link your actions and tactics together. Let's get started.

OBSTACLES

What is standing in the way of improving our talent **RECRUITMENT**? Do we have the right metrics and processes in place to improve our results?

List
- Example: Time, Money, Talent, Experience. . .

OPPORTUNITIES

What operational opportunities will advance our **RECRUITMENT** efforts?

List
- Example: Better Benefits Package, Hybrid Work Environment. . .

THE RIGHT TOOLS TO FIND THE RIGHT CANDIDATES

You're doing a disservice to yourself, your organization, and the person you're recruiting if there isn't clarity on several levels—before you formalize a relationship—because it's expensive to replace a hire, customarily about six to nine months' salary to find a better fit and train them.

The same rules apply if you're seeking internal talent. You've got a great salesperson who seems like they could make a move to sales manager, or a talented engineer who could lead the engineering team. After all, this person has almost all the tools, and you could save yourself six or nine months of hunting.

Historically, recruiting has been about filling a role. HALO makes it about strategy and ensuring that the talent you're considering isn't just qualified in terms of their skills and experience, but aligned with your culture and mission.

Personas. In chapter 3, I discussed personas in detail as part of conceptualizing your external audiences, and the same principles can be applied to talent acquisition. For example, one of the largest healthcare organizations in the country reached out to us for help finding salespeople who were skilled in working with seniors. It was music to my ears when the HR director said, "We don't just want to recruit people, we want the right people with the right **RELATIONSHIPS**." When I asked them if they'd ever developed internal personas around key positions and top performers, there was about 15 seconds of silence. When I asked them if they'd ever detailed the employee journey, again, silence. After the meeting, we spent a week helping them develop personas for that specific sales role, and it looked something like the table on the following page.

SALES REP PERSONA ANALYSIS: XYZ HEALTHCARE

Who are they?	Veteran sales representatives with specific experience in working with seniors. Ideally, they have worked for a regional healthcare organization of similar size to XYZ. Insurance experience a plus. Should have similar skills/experience/personality to our current top rep Chris P.
What questions do they have?	What is the compensation structure? How much travel is involved? How are territories decided? What is the sales manager's style?
What are their pain points?	Uncertainty in the healthcare industry. Many of them have had to job hop to stay employed. Feeling treated like "they're only as good as their last sale."
What do they want?	Basic organizational and financial stability, clarity around quotas, commissions, and bonuses commensurate with performance.

Within the next three months, they had filled all of their vacant sales positions and never again hesitated when someone asked them about the employee journey.

CAMP. Within the HALO framework, one of the key tools is the CAMP system, defined as follows:

- *C=Clarity. What is the job description/role?*

- *A=Accountability. What are the areas that you are accountable for?*

- *M=Metrics/Measurements. What are the metrics and data that we're going to measure you against? What is the definition of success?*

- *P=Performance. What is the cadence that we're going to track and review your performance over time?*

By discussing this concept in detail during the *RECRUITMENT* process—rather than only the job tasks, salary, and benefits—you are giving candidates a much more useful understanding of how your business operates, what their expectations will be, and how they can be successful. In my own business, conveying the CAMP system to potential employees gives them a better idea of what they'll be accountable for, in a less rigid format than a traditional job description.

Internal NPS. HALO practitioners are encouraged to use what we call an internal NPS (Net Promoter Score) for *RECRUITMENT* and *RETENTION*. In the market research world, NPS is used to quantify customer loyalty by dividing survey respondents into promoters, passives, or detractors. Used for internal purposes, an NPS enables you to take the temperature of team members, balancing the interpersonal *RELATIONSHIPS* with their professional capabilities and job performance.

Marketing initiatives. As noted above, marketing can create campaigns about career opportunities at your company that will drive leads. The HALO framework encourages use of the marketing department in other facets too. They can assist in refining what you're looking for and coming up with better job descriptions in a way that helps potential candidates self-select and thus makes the resumes easier to sift through. I'd add that one underutilized marketing capability is to have them help you formulate better interview questions—writers and marketers typically have that skill set, so why not use it?

Job boards. For commodity-type jobs, there's no harm in leaning on job aggregators such as ZipRecruiter or Indeed. This is particularly true if you're an established, well-known brand, and people have heard good things and are eager to work for you. But you also need to accept that the shotgun approach guarantees that you're going to receive hundreds of resumes that you need to wade through. That can add up to a significant waste of your resources—and that's why HALO tools such as personas, CAMP, and the three V's should be introduced as early in the process as possible to ensure cultural match.

Leadership identification. Direct comparisons between business and the military are often overwrought, but let's face it: No one has more demand for effective leadership than Navy SEALs who exist in life-or-death scenarios. The chart pictured below is one of their baseline tools used in identifying potential leaders:

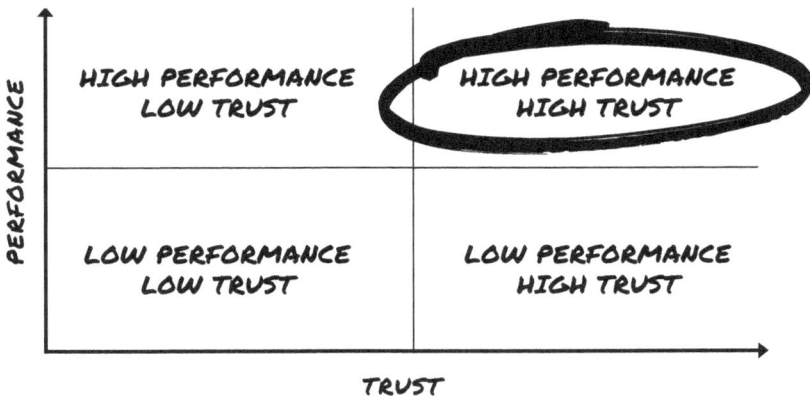

Even if someone is in one of the high-performance boxes, scoring in one of the low-trust boxes will prevent them from moving forward in leadership. Someone who is a low performer but high trust can still take the leadership track with further development. It's always an enlightening exercise when I work with executive teams doing HALO and have them plot where their leaders fall. While it's arguably an anecdotal assessment rather than an analytical one, it's a quick way to identify potential or lack of it.

A secondary related exercise is to plot leadership on the following scale:

Decision Making:

COWARD ←———————————————————→ RECKLESS

COURAGE

Communication:

COWARD ←———————————————————→ RECKLESS

COURAGE

As visually indicated, courage is the midpoint between cowardice and reckless-ness. (While Ryan Holiday's *Courage Is Calling* has popularized this concept for modern readers, it goes all the way back to ancient Greek philosopher Aristotle.) Obviously, being courageous is the ideal: Confident decision making, not afraid to speak up and deal with difficult tasks, and not running and hiding when bad things happen. In reality, very few leaders will fall cleanly into the courageous bucket; indeed, being a bit more reticent or chaotic could be an asset in some circumstances. But as a simple heuristic, this is another worthwhile tool to assess the balance of your team.

Above all, those two exercises can spark a brainstorming session of the key attributes that your company needs. In an ideal world, what's the leader type that we'd want to replicate throughout our organization? The answer depends on your anatomy and your future state, but combining high performance, high trust, courage, and clear communication is the target you should be shooting for.

On a final note, any **RECRUITMENT** strategy you deploy needs to deliver ROI. For years, one of my clients participated in a major industry job fair as a recruiting tool. In addition to spending the money to be a headline sponsor, they sent a team of eight people to Las Vegas to participate in the event. The sponsorship ran about $40,000 a year, and when I asked them to add in the cost of the time for the staff to attend, airfare, hotels, and all-you-can-eat shrimp cocktail, the total came to almost $3 million over the 15 years they participated.

How many people did they recruit from this effort? I'm glad you asked. One. Is that person still working for the company? No.

I know that sounds crazy, but it's an all-too-common error in the **RECRUITMENT** space.

A HALO Perspective on the Interviewing Process

There are thousands (maybe tens of thousands) of books about interviewing, but the finer points of interviewing technique are beyond the scope of this book. There are personal nuances to how each of us prefers to conduct interviews, not to mention the industry you're in and the position you're hiring for. A few overarching concepts, however, can be discussed in terms of the HALO framework.

Interviewer roles. At HALO, I don't meet a candidate until they've worked their way through the ranks. That's not because I believe I'm special, but because what my team is looking for—performance capabilities and skills—is different from what I am looking for. Just because a potential hire checks all of your boxes doesn't mean they check every box for their peers. As your company grows and you get more distant from the trenches, it's even more essential to trust your team's judgment on the more granular aspects of the job. They know what they need.

My role during the interview process is to look at the personality aspects, as far as who the candidate will interact with above, below, and side to side on the org chart—and externally, if it's a client-facing role. I'm trying to ensure a person fits with our culture, because I've learned from experience how damaging it is to make mistakes on that. As I'm sure you'd guess, I rely on the three V's for this process, getting to the heart of what their personal values are and what makes them feel valued as an employee. As part of the evaluation, I'll ask questions such as:

- *What makes you feel valued?*
- *What are your personal values?*
- *What value do you believe you can add to the organization?*
- *Do you feel valued based on your compensation?*
- *Does it make you feel valued if you're praised in front of your peers?*
- *Do you feel valued if your manager gives you personal attention?*

Personal connections. Especially for high-impact roles, the vetting process is the formative stage of a relationship—and that means spending time with a candidate outside the office environment, meeting for a cup of coffee or lunch. Bottom line, they need to pass the airplane test: Would you mind sitting in the middle seat next to this person for five hours, or would you be reaching for a parachute and the emergency exit lever? I don't care if they're the most talented person ever, you ignore those types of red flags at your peril.

Behavioral assessments. I don't want to dismiss the various types of personality tests, whether Myers-Briggs, DiSC, Predictive Index, or any of the others, because they can be helpful in certain scenarios. What they don't take into account is what your vision of success is, what business stage you're in, or where you're trying to get to. You might require someone with certain behavioral characteristics—detail oriented, aggressive, etc.—and those don't necessarily come across in every test. I've also seen companies squander the results by failing to put them into action with tracking and measuring. At that point, you're just throwing a couple thousand bucks into the void, and it's no more valuable than a pub game.

In a similar vein, there's a popular test for choosing leadership positions that one of our clients was using to help pick their new CEO. When it came down to the final two candidates, I strongly preferred one while the method was recommending the other. Truth be told, if they used that candidate, they would probably be fine. But the issue is that it wasn't taking into account what was required for the desired growth path, getting from the current state to the future state—and that would require a very specific type of person. A boilerplate fill-in-the-dot test is never a proper substitute for human judgment.

In 2023, Monster.com published a Workplace Red Flags survey[13] that identified a number of interviewing process pain points for job seekers. What were the biggest red flags?

- *65% of respondents consider jobs that require more than three rounds of interviews the biggest red flag in the process.*

- *40% said not disclosing a salary range in the job description would prevent them from applying.*

- *53% said a mandatory assignment would prevent them from applying.*

DON'T COMPOUND YOUR PROBLEMS

You're surely familiar with the old saying, "Hire for attitude, train for skill." That sounds nice in principle, but context is everything. In the recent past, I've seen large companies make major mistakes, hiring people they like, who are solid team players, to roles for which they're completely unqualified. One company wanted to move someone from managing warehouses to overseeing business intelligence. Another thought a recent college graduate could run their marketing department—and even worse, they were trying to save money by making them an intern instead of an employee. When I flat out asked the CEO, "Do you really want an intern to own marketing for your $40 million business?" he quickly said no and we moved on. Mercifully, in both cases I was able to persuade them their plans weren't the prudent path for their growth aspirations.

But it underscores the issue that transcends companies of all sizes and industries. If you don't understand what your needs are, or if you allow the process to be anecdotal not analytical, you are going to run into problems.

---

13   https://hiring.monster.com/resources/blog/
       monster-poll-micromanagement-is-the-biggest-workplace-red-flag

If you hire a person who's bad for a role, good people are going to head for the exit because they're frustrated and can't deal with incompetence. Quality starts to drop. Your customer feedback ratings start to fall. Your workforce loses its mojo and more good people leave. You start getting lousy reviews on Glassdoor, which affects your ability to recruit. Oh, and when a poor performer is in any kind of managerial role, there's a 100% chance that they will subsequently hire other underperformers. It becomes a perpetual cycle that all started with poor hiring practices.

It's a worst-case scenario. I've made this mistake myself, long before I developed HALO and the CAMP process. I hired people who I was confident would be a good fit, and they weren't. Compounding the problem, I didn't provide clarity, didn't create personas, didn't offer them a vision of success or the metrics to get there. Like many entrepreneurs and executives in my position, I used the excuse that I didn't have the time. But the truth was that I just didn't want to do the work. Impatience, a let's-get-this-done attitude can serve a purpose in growing your business, but it's counterproductive when you're dealing with **RECRUITMENT**. Hiring the wrong person is what slows everything down. Looking back, it was unfair to the employee as well. I own that.

How do you get out of this vicious circle? I've mentioned Officevibe several times in this book, and again I'll point to it as a valuable tool. Whether Officevibe or any kind of internal NPS system, you need to have a way for people to give feedback on the chemistry of your operation. While individual bad employee reviews are beyond your immediate control, it's a darn good incentive to create a better atmosphere in your company through better recruiting.

Success Breeds Success

In some respects, **RECRUITMENT** is the broccoli of the 6R's. It's easy to look at items like **REVENUE, RELATIONSHIPS,** or **RECOGNITION** and believe that they're the biggest pain point—while the underlying cause is a defective **RECRUITMENT** process. **RECRUITMENT** isn't just the least sexy of the R's, it often involves the most daunting drudge work and intense activity. If you're the executive or the entrepreneur, and you yourself do not know what you need, it's unfair to put that on the people that you hire, people that you recruit.

Also consider the bigger picture: Recruiting is a commitment that both parties are making, both at the corporate level and by the prospective employee, to do our best work and live our best lives. This is what people are looking for, and what companies are looking for as well. When you start to look at it that way, you begin to view your **RECRUITMENT** strategy as a way to build value for yourself and others.

For some employees, a job is just a job. They don't aspire for a higher position or think of what they're doing as a career; they just want to pay the bills. And that's OK. But key positions deserve the bulk of your attention.

If you think about dominant basketball teams like the Chicago Bulls in the 1990s, Michael Jordan would come to mind—even if you're not a hoops fan like I am. But the reason the Bulls were a dynasty is because the general managers and coaches understood the need for harmony. Jordan wouldn't have won championships without role players like Scottie Pippen, Dennis Rodman, and Steve Kerr, among many others, because they balanced him out. The same rules apply for companies: If you put all your focus on **REVENUE** (i.e., Jordan), you'll score a lot of points in the short term at the cost of long-term growth.

By putting a more strategic effort into blending leadership excellence with strength of your role players, **RECRUITMENT** can become a difference maker. Like a pro sports dynasty, business success breeds success, and that **REPUTATION** will help attract and retain more talent too. Like the Navy SEALs, whose mantra is "Slow is Smooth, Smooth is Fast," a methodical, deliberate approach to recruiting will inevitably be the quickest route to a positive outcome.

Once you've got the right people in the right seats, your mission turns to the topic of our next R: **RETENTION**.

To download a fillable PDF version of the exercises
in this chapter, visit *haloforall.com/hrh*

Six Key Takeaways

1. **Revenue** happens when you fill a role with someone who not only has the right skills and experience—they're aligned with your culture and mission too.

2. Hiring is easy. Recruiting is hard.

3. The quality of your hires is going to directly impact your ability to drive more **Revenue**, top-line and bottom-line earnings.

4. If you don't understand what your needs are, or if you allow the process to be anecdotal not analytical, you are going to run into problems.

5. Recruiting is a commitment that both parties are making, both at the corporate level and by the prospective employee, to do our best work and live our best lives.

6. By putting a more strategic effort into blending leadership excellence with strength of your role players, **Recruitment** can become a difference maker.

"PROFITS ARE RELATED TO CUSTOMER RETENTION. CUSTOMER RETENTION IS RELATED TO EMPLOYEE RETENTION."

— JEFFREY PFEFFER

CHAPTER 8

RETENTION:

TALENT AND CUSTOMER DEVELOPMENT

How to measure and nurture internal and external
Relationships so that you're fostering loyalty.

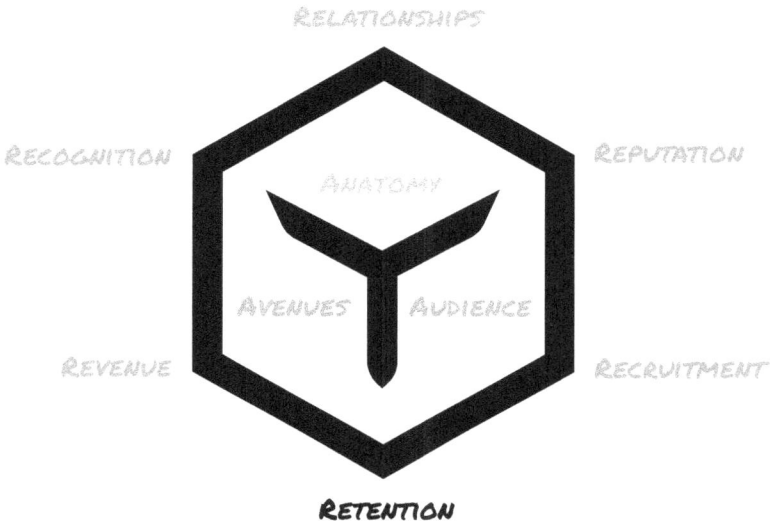

RELATIONSHIPS

RECOGNITION

REPUTATION

ANATOMY

AVENUES   AUDIENCE

REVENUE

RECRUITMENT

RETENTION

The executive team of a midsize client and I were gathered around a conference room table, seated in comfy black leather chairs, with the afternoon sun streaming through the windows. They'd been experiencing a significant exodus of valuable employees, and the day's mission was to find out why that was happening and what to do about it.

While **RETENTION** was the immediate item on the agenda, I needed to grab their attention—because my intuition was that the situation was more dire than they realized. "Before we drill down into root causes and how to fix them, can you estimate what this problem is costing you every year?" I asked.

After some hemming and hawing, no one had anything resembling an answer. I paused, and looked at the large whiteboard on the wall, but grabbed a white legal pad and pen instead. "OK, let's see what we're dealing with," I said. "How many employees do you have?"

I scribbled the number on my pad. "Great. And what's your annual turnover rate?" I asked.

Another quick squiggle. "Last but not least, what's the blended average salary and benefits for your typical employee?" I said. "A round number is fine—doesn't need to be down to the nearest penny."

Again, I wrote down the number, then took 30 seconds to do the calculation.

- *NUMBER OF EMPLOYEES: 740*
- *AVERAGE SALARY: $125,000*
- *YEARLY TURNOVER RATE: 12%*
- *YEARLY COST OF TURNOVER:*

$11.1 MILLION

I showed them the paper. As you can see, their **RETENTION** problem was costing them about $11 million a year.

A few of them sat there, expressionless. Others were sharpening their pitchforks. "No, that's bullshit," the HR director said, visibly angered. "Absolutely not."

Although they disagreed with my math, it was obvious that they needed to quantify the cost. They convened an internal team to do some research.

Fast forward 14 weeks. It turned out that I was wrong. The actual cost was $10.6 million.

Regardless of the math, this story isn't about how close I came or the thrill of a gotcha. It's the fact that far too few companies, even larger ones, fully comprehend the financial implications of **RETENTION**. Retaining quality people is essential for building your **REPUTATION**, cultivating sustainable **RELATIONSHIPS**, and increasing **RECOGNITION**—and of course driving **REVENUE** and profitability. (As we'll discuss, the same principles apply to customers and clients.) When you identify the cost of the problem, it puts a fine point on why you need to make changes. In the case of this company, we ended up creating a six-page document that was solely focused on their people strategy for the next 10 years.

In full disclosure, I don't believe that the client or I captured the full costs of their **RETENTION** problem in our respective calculations. Why? The real damage is losing your high performers who are growth minded and aligned with your core values—visionary thinkers who aren't just looking to solve a problem, but to make the solution part of your DNA. When high-skilled workers drop a resignation letter on your desk, you're losing the people who win the work, build the systems, create the innovations, and ensure the quality of your products and services. There's a camaraderie component too: One's peers are key to **RETENTION**, and top performers want to be surrounded by other top performers.

In a worst-case scenario, you might be forced to replace them with the wrong people and exacerbate your problems.

Maybe it doesn't add a zero to your $X million or thousands, but over the long haul, lost talent can be devastating to the organization in ways that don't immediately show up on a spreadsheet.

Look, a Bonus Exercise!

We'll get to defining **RETENTION** and our regular HALO exercises shortly. Before we do, I encourage you to put this book down for a few minutes to tackle two tasks:

- Take out a scratch paper and do the **RETENTION**-cost calculation described above.

- **ANSWER THIS QUESTION:** What is the hidden domino effect of losing good people and recruiting poor performers in your organization?

What Is Retention?

RETENTION involves internal and external efforts aimed at keeping the right people within an organization and keeping clients engaged with an organization's products and services. At the risk of stating the obvious, if you lose too many customers, you're in trouble. If you lose your best people, you're in even more trouble. But the math and strategy behind figuring out what's happening is sometimes a lot more complex.

On the employee side, a strategic **RETENTION** effort allows a company not only to keep employees who are critical to the success of the business, but avoid the financial costs associated with employee turnover. Estimates for the cost of a lost employee range from six to nine months' salary to more than 200% for a highly skilled worker.

On the customer or client side, **RETENTION** is vital to developing a lasting and consistent **REVENUE** stream, while reducing the costs associated with customer churn and acquisition. It doesn't matter if you're B2B, D2C, B2C, or B2G, nor does it make a difference where you are in your maturity stage. Customer service plays a huge role in your **RETENTION**, and your own personal experience probably testifies how fast people will abandon your product or service if the experience is below their expectations. Statistics indicate the cost of obtaining a new customer can be three to 25 times the expense of retaining an existing one.

Since **RETENTION** is both an internal and an external effort, it requires internal initiatives headed up by the HR and leadership teams and external initiatives led by the sales, marketing, customer service, and leadership teams. In both cases, **RETENTION** relies heavily on **RELATIONSHIPS**, leaning on the ability to illustrate value to customers or the feeling of being valued to employees. How well a company does with **RETENTION** invariably impacts its **REPUTATION** and, inevitably, its **REVENUE**.

In most cases, external **RETENTION** efforts will focus on the benefits of a company's products or services. Internal **RETENTION** efforts should focus on the benefits an employee receives, salary and beyond. In other words, both are value-based initiatives. As is the case with **REPUTATION**, **RETENTION** is among the 6R's that truly span the entire enterprise in a holistic way. In terms of leading the initiatives, however, the breakdown is generally as follows:

TALENT RETENTION

- *Leadership*
- *Human Resources*

CLIENT/CUSTOMER RETENTION

- *Leadership*
- *Marketing*
- *Sales/Business Development*
- *Customer Service*

What Metrics Should I Use to Measure Retention?

Generally speaking, the **RETENTION** of both employees and clients/customers should be addressed with a combination of two strategies: satisfaction metrics (formal, structured surveys or other measurements) and pulse checks (immediate "check-in"-style reactions in business meetings and after purchase decisions).

Talent Retention

Measuring talent **RETENTION** can run the gamut, but here are a few examples commonly used by HALO practitioners:

- *Employee satisfaction score (#,%)*
- *Internal net promoter score (#,%)*
- *Voluntary turnover (#,%)*
- *Involuntary turnover (#,%)*
- *CAMP (#,%)*

Client/Customer Retention

How you measure this type of **RETENTION** depends on the type of business you're in. A few examples:

Service-Based Businesses

- *Long-term surveys (#,%)*
- *Post-meeting surveys (#,%)*
- *Average client longevity (#,%)*
- *Net promoter score (#)*
- *Client satisfaction score (#,%)*
- *Churn rate (%)*

PRODUCT-BASED BUSINESSES

- *Social listening/online reviews (#,%)*
- *Pop-up post-purchase surveys (#,%)*
- *Membership signups/renewals (#,%)*
- *Website/in-person visits (#,%)*
- *Subscriptions (#,%)*
- *Email open rate (%)*
- *Repeat purchases (#,%)*
- *Net promoter score (#)*
- *Client satisfaction score (#,%)*
- *Churn rate (%)*

WHERE DO YOU STAND WHEN IT COMES TO RETENTION?

EXERCISE #1   **Pain Scale**

You know the drill by now. Ask your team to discuss the definition of **RETENTION**, and then have each participant circle the face that describes their feeling about your company's current state.

Important: This is one of those occasions where you'll want to do at least two pain scales: one externally for **RETENTION** of customers/clients and one internally for employees. Depending on your circumstance, you can also repeat these exercises for your strategic partners.

RETENTION

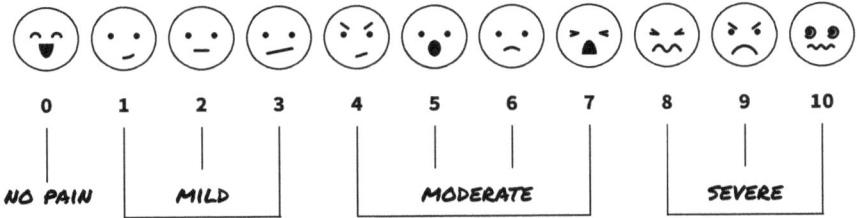

0	1	2	3	4	5	6	7	8	9	10

NO PAIN | **MILD** | **MODERATE** | **SEVERE**

With that done, collect the worksheets, total the numbers, average them, and enter the number in the pain scale hexagon matrix on page 179.

As with the previous R's, If the overall pain-scale average is six or higher, or if the opinions are divergent, I encourage conducting a deeper discussion with your team.

EXERCISE #2 **Obstacles and Opportunities**

During your discussion, please consider both your current tactics (what are we currently doing to build **RETENTION**?) and future strategy (how can increasing our **RETENTION** lead to future **REVENUE**-generating opportunities?). For maximum business impact, this exercise should be performed separately for your internal and external audiences.

The Obstacles/Opportunities process is designed to link your actions and tactics together. Let's go.

OBSTACLES – INTERNAL

What is standing in the way of improving **RETENTION** with our high performers? Do we have the right metrics and processes in place to improve our talent **RETENTION**?

List
- Example: Time, Money, Talent, Experience. . .

OBSTACLES – EXTERNAL

What is standing in the way of building the **RETENTION** needed to grow our business with our customers/clients? Do we have the right metrics and processes in place to improve our **RETENTION**?

List
- Example: Time, Money, Talent, Experience. . .

OPPORTUNITIES - INTERNAL

What operational opportunities will help build **RETENTION** within our workforce?

List
- Example: Time, Money, Talent, Experience. . .

OPPORTUNITIES - EXTERNAL

What operational opportunities will help build client or customer **RETENTION**?

List
- Example: Time, Money, Talent, Experience. . .

Reminder: Although human resources may take the lead on internal initiatives, or sales/marketing/customer service on the external side, **RETENTION** is a factor that affects and is affected by every department! Moreover, each department may have different needs and goals. Consider taking a deeper dive with your HALO group—including an entirely separate session on **RETENTION** within each of the departments.

Keeping Your High Performers

No matter how large and successful a company is, they're not immune from employee **RETENTION** issues. Amazon dominates the world of online retail, and pretty much has its act together. But just a few years ago, they were suffering 180% employee turnover. Yes, they needed to replace their entire staff every six months—an unsustainable path that was causing delayed packages and unhappy customers, decreasing revenue, and allowing competitors such as Walmart to gain market share.

In a bold, decisive move in the second half of 2022, Amazon leadership told their board and shareholders that they were going to invest every dollar of profit for the quarter—about $4 billion—to fix the combined **RETENTION/ RECRUITMENT** problem.

As an entrepreneur or executive, your problem is unlikely to have nine zeros after it like Amazon's—but it's still expensive to replace an employee, and that's not including the psychological pain and disruption within your teams. Whether an initiative is led by HR or another department, the first rule of **RETENTION** Club is to talk about **RETENTION** Club: *We need a Retention strategy for our people.* You know it as well as I do. Holiday parties, ping pong tables, and free gym memberships are fine as far as they go—but they're not a substitute for an actual plan to keep your best people. The real work starts with two questions:

1. Why would someone want to stay at our organization?

2. How do we keep the people that we want to stay at this organization?

As noted in the previous chapter about **RECRUITMENT**, the HALO CAMP principles transfer over into **RETENTION**: You need to have clarity (C) in the job description.

Having accountability (A) is essential for ensuring alignment during the hiring process, but now it transitions into what they're accountable for, using the metrics and measurements (M) you defined. And finally, during the hiring process you discussed performance (P), so you need to stick to the cadence of reviews that were outlined.

Like **RECRUITMENT**, internal **RETENTION** is another piece of broccoli on your plate, and answering those questions is hard. You'd rather munch on something else, even though you know it's good for you. If you're overly focused on driving **REVENUE**, you might think your paying customers are more important than anyone inside your office drawing a salary. But that's not going to last if the quality people who provide your product or service walk out the door.

I've mentioned it before, and I'm obligated to say it again: The difference between being anecdotal and being analytical is the difference between saying *I think* vs. *I know*. This is a critical issue in **RETENTION**; businesses think they know what their people want. It's become even worse with the advent of work from home for companies that want to get their people back in the office, stacking up the amenities, adding free coffee, or catering lunch once a week.

My position: Why don't you just ask your employees what it would take? What is the value of getting them back into the office? What we're also seeing from an organizational standpoint, however, is the back-to-office push is becoming part of the **RETENTION** problem. Unless you're in a business that requires in-person presence, employees want the flexibility of working from home or anywhere. If you're a member of the old guard who craves face time in a business that can be done remotely, I gotta tell ya, that world is likely gone forever.

One approach that can help is the concept of a results-only work environment (ROWE), which can be highly effective in office or remote formats. Such a methodology also fits neatly with the accountability principles of CAMP—and precludes the need to micromanage. By focusing on results, ROWE also aligns with one of the purposes of HALO: shining light into dark corners, enabling you to differentiate between performers and nonperformers. There will be some people who react poorly to that, because it's a threat to their existence. For others, it's an opportunity to develop them further and unlock their potential.

Identifying your high performers (and low performers) is a matter of your individual company culture, and quite honestly it's beyond the scope of this book. There are plenty of options out there; for instance the 9-box grid that many enterprise companies use to cluster people into A, B, and C players. Even in small companies, you need to have a plan for people you want to retain, including those you want to keep but they're in the wrong seat. Over time, I've discovered that it can be as simple as telling high-performing talents that you want to retain them, and maintaining a human connection.

To Retain Talent, Keep Your Eye on the Flags

In 2023, Monster.com published a Workplace Red Flags survey[14] that explored pain points in the workplace that are worth considering as you build out your talent RETENTION strategy. Some of the key findings:

- *73% of workers said micromanagement is the biggest workplace red flag and 46% said micromanagement could be a reason for leaving their job.*

- *If you're trying to create a "fun" environment, be aware that team-bonding exercises (31%) and happy hours (27%) are a pain point for some workers.*

- *51% said rigid 9–5 hours are a pain point, while the same percentage called flexible remote work policies the biggest green flag for a place they'd want to be an employee.*

---

14   https://hiring.monster.com/resources/blog/
       monster-poll-micromanagement-is-the-biggest-workplace-red-flag

RETAINING CLIENTS THROUGH THE INTEGRATED BUSINESS CYCLE

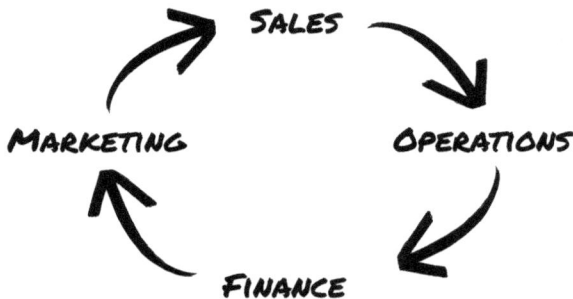

We've all been there. You make the sale. . . and eventually forget about the customer because they're low maintenance and you assume they're satisfied because they're still buying and not complaining. Great, let's move on to the next acquisition. In my ad agency days, I saw it all the time. No matter how successful we were at driving people to the top of someone's funnel, the ones that made it to the bottom didn't always stick around. Eventually, the lightbulb goes on that it's not just about harvesting more leads, building better products, or investing in technology. If people are dropping, there's a flaw in the system somewhere.

INTEGRATED BUSINESS CYCLE

SALES

OPERATIONS

FINANCE

MARKETING

That's why the second part of the HALO *RETENTION* process homes in on clients or customers. In the HALO system, our go-to strategy is to create an integrated business cycle, which is designed to define the entire client experience, from marketing and sales through operations and everything else. The goal is to do a deep dive of processing as many steps as possible, so that you can identify every aspect of the relationship needed to retain the client. (Note, an integrated business cycle can also be deployed for your internal audience if you choose.)

Here's what it looks like from a big-picture perspective:

- **Recognition**: How do we build **RECOGNITION** with a prospect or partner that doesn't know we exist? What does that process look like?

- **Commitment**: How do we provide clarity before they make a commitment to get into a relationship with us?

- **Post-sales relationship:** What is the process of us serving them and moving them into a closer bond, and how can we use that to build our Reputation?

- **Operations:** What are we doing to service that client based on the product or service, and what corrective actions need to be taken when needed?

- **Recruitment:** Are we sure that we have the right team that's delivering our product or service to that relationship? What are the gaps?

- **Retention:** What processes do we have in place so a customer becomes loyal, and how might we evolve them into an advocate? Are our employees being kept accountable to the right metrics?

The integrated business cycle system is designed to thoroughly outline and process each of those steps and—here's the most important part—put systems in place where there need to be checkpoints. External examples might include a periodic measurement or metric to ensure that the relationship is positive, or commissioning a feedback survey on the experience with marketing and sales, and then associating it with the value to future **REVENUE**. Internally, it can include items such as tracking the satisfaction of recruits and the **RETENTION** figures, and regular check-ins to see how employees are feeling.

The end result is a systemized process that's efficient and effective, because it's injecting accountability into every stage of the relationship, and even giving you the timing where everything is supposed to happen. In addition, it's a replicable process—any time you add a new client or start a new division, just plug and play. (Stay tuned to more discussion on this when we arrive at the Execute section.)

One of the key elements of the integrated business cycle approach is the concept of pulse checks, particularly for service-oriented businesses. It could be a quick call to a client to ask how everything's going. Maybe it's a one-question survey after every meeting: "Are you satisfied?" or "Are we meeting expectations?"—and we've even got HALO clients who repurpose the pain scale you've seen in the exercises for that purpose. Based on the answers of your communications, you'll have opportunities to read the signs and head off potential problems early in the process.

In chapter 5, I briefly discussed the importance of knowing and tracking your customer lifetime value; in brief, the average relationship duration times the expected **REVENUE**. At the **RETENTION** stage, you start to understand why that calculation is so vital. If you have a $100,000 client, it could cost you $300,000 or more to replace them, between the marketing spend and people you need to hire to secure them. Even worse, every time you onboard a new client, you're starting from scratch. With a newbie, there's a lot more handholding and you don't speak the same language the way you do with a longtime client.

Finally, success in customer/client **RETENTION** is about maintaining the *right* **RELATIONSHIPS**. As is the case with low-performing employees, you could have a paying customer who absorbs too many of your resources. That's a wrong relationship, and it's not good for your mental health, nor the health of your teams and overall business. Customer service needs to maintain only those strong **RELATIONSHIPS** that you want to perpetuate, by focusing on service and engagement that results in sustainable growth.

A Lesson in Retention. . . the Hard Way

The most important **RETENTION** lesson of my career came in the form of a rockstar graphic designer, let's call her Beth. We'd been making changes at the agency and had doubled in size, and I was becoming less involved in the day to day of the business. That was great for me, but not for her. Unwittingly, I'd hired a person above Beth who wasn't an ideal manager, and an assistant designer below her who didn't have the right skill set. When I'd ask her how things were going, though, she'd tell me everything was great and that she loved working for our agency.

Like so many business owners, I overlooked the fact that people don't always want to be honest with us, not least because it could jeopardize their job. Well, when we started using Officevibe, I was able to piece together that Beth wasn't telling me the truth. Her utilization levels were higher than they should be, indicating she was doing more work than she should, and her stress levels were high too.

When I realized the situation, I popped into Beth's office and sat down. "I feel like you're not telling me everything," I said. "I want to know what's going on, because I care about you as a person, and I care about retaining you. You're incredibly valuable to me."

That's when she started to cry. She didn't like working for her new manager, and she felt like she was having to rework too much of the assistant designer's output. Beth admitted she was within a month or two of quitting. Hearing the feedback and confident she wasn't the problem—that was all me, with my failure to hire properly—I let the other two people go. I knew they were wrong for the positions and this was the push I needed to make the change. I also let Beth know that I'd be there for her when she was ready to move on.

It was a stark reminder that many people are going to tell you what they think you want to hear, especially those who are quiet and diligent by nature. It was also a reminder of how risky that can be for an entrepreneur, or to an executive who's trying to build a business. As soon as you walk away, someone might be polishing their resume. More important, it made me realize that I needed to develop a strategy. It's easy to spot a problem employee, whether they're whining about parking or the coffee creamer flavors in the kitchenette. With quiet performers, you can fool yourself into thinking everything's A-OK.

In retrospect, it required me to do a better job of understanding her own three V's—and to do the same for every other person in the office. Even though I valued her, Beth had gotten to the point where she no longer felt valued, and the value of the job wasn't there anymore either. After we removed the people above and below her, the three V's and her Officevibe scores went back into balance.

The epilogue to the story is that Beth worked for me for another 18 months, far happier and still one of the top creative talents I've ever encountered. Even when she came to tell me she was leaving, she emphasized that it was mostly about the opportunity to specialize in user interface design, which our agency didn't do much of at that time. I told her I understood, and that I'd gladly serve as a reference and help her vet the agencies she was considering.

Beth is thriving at her new company, just like I knew she would. I also know that if I ever had the right job, she'd come back and work for me in a heartbeat. To me, retaining the relationship that I have with her is the best kind of *RETENTION* you can get.

That's enough broccoli for now. In the next chapter we'll move on to a very different kind of green, the final of the 6R's: *REVENUE*.

To download a fillable PDF version of the exercises
in this chapter, visit *haloforall.com/hrh*

Six Key Takeaways

1. **REVENUE** happens when your strategies focus on retaining
   high performers who are growth minded and aligned with your
   core values.

2. Two of the most important metrics for every executive to know are
   churn rate (customer loss) and turnover (employee loss).

3. To improve those metrics, **RETENTION** relies on internal initiatives
   led by the HR and leadership teams and external initiatives led by
   the sales/marketing, customer service, and leadership teams.

4. Estimates for the cost of a lost employee range from six to nine
   months' salary to more than 200% for a highly skilled worker.

5. The cost of obtaining a new customer is five to 25 the expense of
   retaining an existing one.

6. The **RETENTION** stage underscores why you must absolutely know
   your customer lifetime value—so you are aware of the risks.

"Companies that
get confused, that
think their goal is
revenue or stock
Price. You have to
focus on the things
that lead to those."

—Tim Cook

CHAPTER 9

REVENUE:
THE RESULT, NOT THE DESTINATION

Increasing what you bring in, reducing what you
waste, and reinvesting your profits holistically.

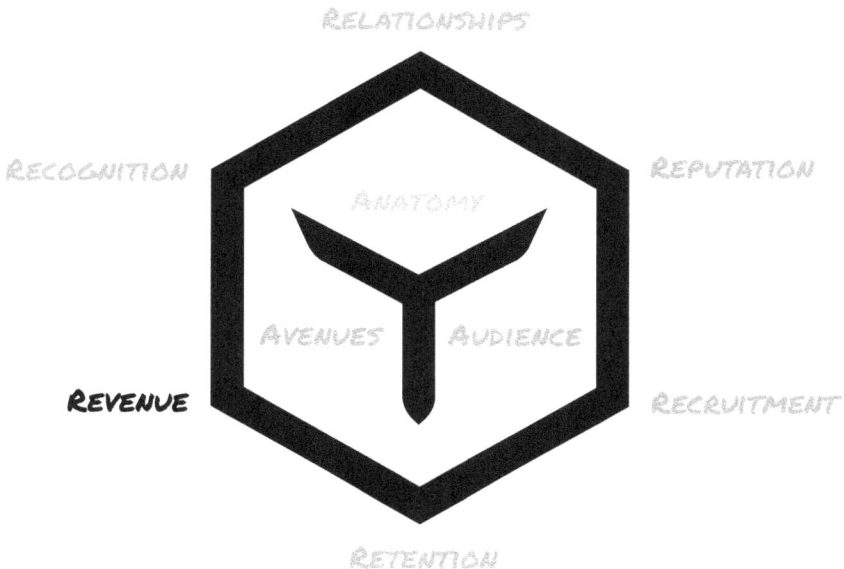

When you were in high school, it probably sounded cool to work in an ice cream shop—but if you had any friends who did, I guarantee they couldn't stand to look at a banana split by the end of the summer. As we grow into adults, it often evolves into dreams about starting a restaurant, a bed and breakfast in Vermont, or a fitness studio.

Sure, those seem like inherently fun businesses, doing something that you and other people enjoy. Then reality sets in.

The microbrewery business is something that falls into that category, and one of our HALO clients was trying to actualize her dreams. As one of only a handful of female brewers in the country, Anne was already an underdog. She was brewing some fantastic beers, and people loved them. But her revenues weren't what she needed them to be, and the business side was a never-ending struggle despite the popularity.

As we combed through her books, we identified one of the main problems: the profitability of the individual beer SKUs. Anne knew how many barrels of each beer had been going out, but she was making anecdotal decisions about what to brew and when and where to sell it. Even though she was selling more beer, her revenues weren't increasing as much as they should. Her decision making was based on her intuition—in other words, what she thought, not what she knew.

Pulling together all of Anne's sales data created a lightbulb moment, since she had never looked at her products that way. Now she's able to make data-driven decisions and have confidence in how sales are going to affect her revenues. It also enables her to cut expenses, because she can look at the profitability of individual beers and identify which ones have the higher probability of sales in different establishments or stores.

Armed with the right metrics and data, Anne was able to increase her overall revenues by 65% within the first year of implementing HALO. This solid financial footing gave her the freedom to explore new avenues for her creativity. She now had the confidence to test out new beer flavors, with the reduced risk afforded by her data-driven decisions.

Mind you, this isn't just an obstacle or opportunity for small businesses. I've worked with plenty of midsize and enterprise-level companies that haven't embraced data to understand their business efficiency, make decisions, or identify what's going to move the needle.

WHAT IS REVENUE?

When initially discussing the 6R's and prioritizing pain points, most people instinctively assume that **REVENUE** is the top item they need to address—after all, more income would solve a lot of problems. By the end of the HALO process, they understand how **REVENUE** is important, but it's the result, not the destination. **REVENUE** happens when you build the other R's.

As business owners, we're typically obsessed with **REVENUE**—it's our oxygen. But think of it as the difference between being a hunter and a farmer. Successfully stalking an animal will feed you and your family for a time, but then you have winter, droughts, or even just bad luck in the field. In contrast, if you perfect how you cultivate and store food, if you pay attention to the whole ecosystem, you'll have consistent nourishment, always and forever.

It happens all the time when I ask a businessperson how it's going. "It's feast or famine," I'll hear. "Either we're crazy busy or we've got nothing going on." By focusing on harmony and balance through the 6R's, you can make sure the peaks and valleys are not as dramatic. Not only does it make your business more predictable, it makes your business—and you, as a leader!—more manageable.

All of the R's relate to **REVENUE** as a whole and the reason why we're doing all this isn't for short-term **REVENUE** gain. It's about long-term, sustainable, and predictable **REVENUE**. That's what's going to help us get over those humps of being overworked, overwhelmed, and underperforming.

But you also need to dig one step deeper. Beyond top-line revenues and bottom-line earnings, we want to consider how we're using our **REVENUE**—in particular, how we're reinvesting it holistically and spending those dollars in order to grow forward.

What Metrics Should I Use to Measure Revenue?

Not everyone arrives into the business world with a financial background. Moreover, items such as top-line revenue, bottom-line earnings, profitability, ratios, P&Ls, cash flow, budgets, and forecasting—and on and on—are highly dependent on your individual business. Whether you use spreadsheets, Tableau, QuickBooks, or a proprietary accounting program, a detailed discussion of your corporate finances is beyond the scope of this book. (Keep in mind, even many books about corporate finance tell you what to do when you have the revenue, but not how **REVENUE** happens—which is the holy grail of HALO.)

Instead, let's take a HALO framework perspective on the high-level figures you need to be conversant with—even if your accountant, CPA, or finance department is handling the actual duties. We use the acronym CORE, with slightly different meanings depending on your business stage.

Early-stage Companies

- **C=CASH POSITION.** If you're a small business owner or entrepreneur, you might have $25,000 in your checking account. That's your cash position today, and you want to grow it to $100,000.

- **O=OPERATING COSTS.** In addition to the cash position, you need (for example) three to five months of operating costs to be in your comfort zone. Your operational overhead simply means what it costs for you to run your business today, but you also need to know where you want it to be in the future. A very basic example would be a company that wants a maximum of 55% of their revenues going towards salaries and overhead, which allows them to generate 15% profitability.

- **R=REVENUE.** What is the top-line revenue number currently and where do you want to get to? It's essential to be realistic. If you generated $500,000 last year, you might be able to double it this year, but $5 million is probably a reach.

- **E=EARNINGS.** What is your profit, both in percentage and in dollar amount? What is a reasonable target for growing your business?

MATURE COMPANIES

- **C=CAPEX.** A capital expenditure (a.k.a., capital expense) is money used to purchase, maintain, or expand fixed assets. These are long-term expenditures, intended to be used for more than a year.

- **O=OPEX.** As with early-stage companies, this number is your operating expenses, including salaries, rent or mortgage payments, utilities, and property taxes.

- **R=REVENUE.** See above

- **E=EARNINGS.** See above

While this is one of the shorter chapters in this book, it's not because **REVENUE** isn't important, or that it's not one of your pain points.

There are only three ways to grow your revenues:

- *Charge more for your product or service.*

- *Bring on more customers for your product or service.*

- *Cut the expenses required to create your product or deliver your service.*

It's that simple. If you want to do all three, you can do that—but the five other R's need to be there to help you sustain and grow your returns. Can we just start raising prices? Perhaps, but that might lead to **RETENTION** problems for your customer base. How do we get more customers? You build **RECOGNITION** with them. Where can we cut expenses? Be mindful that it doesn't harm your quality in a way that undermines your **REPUTATION** or **RELATIONSHIPS**. The only way you will know is if you're tracking the metrics that matter most for your business.

WHERE DO YOU STAND WHEN IT COMES TO REVENUE?

EXERCISE #1   ## Pain Scale

One more time. Have your team discuss the definition of **REVENUE**, and then have each participant circle the face that describes their feeling about your company's current state.

REVENUE

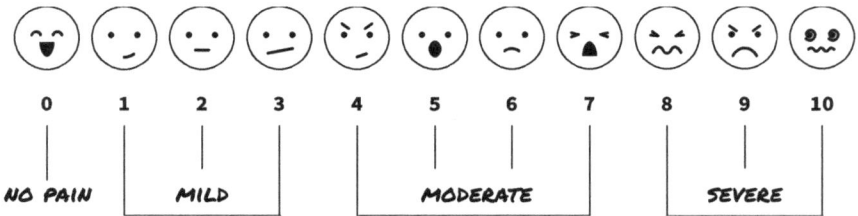

With that done, collect the worksheets, total the numbers, average them, and enter the number in the pain scale hexagon matrix on page 179.

As with the previous R's, If the overall pain-scale average is six or higher, or if the opinions are divergent, I encourage conducting a deeper discussion with your team.

EXERCISE #2   ## Obstacles and Opportunities

During your discussion, please consider both your current tactics (what are we currently doing to improve revenue generation?) and future strategy (how can we create future revenue-generating opportunities?).

The Obstacles/Opportunities process is designed to link your actions and tactics together. Let's get started.

OBSTACLES

What is standing in the way of improving our **REVENUE**? Do we have the right metrics and processes in place to improve our results?

List
- Example: Time, Money, Talent, Experience...

OPPORTUNITIES

What operational opportunities will advance our **REVENUE**?

List
- Finance, Marketing...

EFFICIENCY MATTERS

The integrated business cycle, mentioned in the **RETENTION** chapter, can also play a key role in improving overall efficiency and **REVENUES**. With all of your business groups going through the integrated business cycle process, you can overlay where steps are the same or different and use data to truncate unnecessary steps—squeezing more earnings out of revenue by doing more with less.

For example, imagine you currently have a 20-step process for onboarding a new client. Using technology, you calculate that you can reduce the 20 steps down to 10, which saves 25 person-hours at $100 an hour. Quick math, that means you can recapture $2,500 in resources that hit your bottom line—freeing up that employee to focus on more important tasks. It might be a matter of computerizing a manual process or getting away from using Excel spreadsheets into something more sophisticated such as Tableau. A $10,000 investment in an off-the-shelf system could save $200,000 over three years. Beyond traditional software solutions, the field of artificial intelligence (AI) is already dramatically expanding our concept of what processes can be automated. As we at HALO start to imagine—and launch—tools for the future of work, our LEO AI will help organizations streamline processes and save money. Fingers crossed, by the time you've picked up this book, you might already be benefiting from LEO's help!

Toyota's kaizen process offers a classic example of how minor efficiency tweaks can create a larger impact over time. Snip 1% here and another 1% there, those little things start to compound and stack up. That's one of the key strategies Toyota deployed to grow into the behemoth that it is: by optimizing formerly inefficient processes.

The HALO framework is designed to instill that same mentality, using key measurements to define success and make improvements, automating and optimizing wherever there's an opportunity. But this is important: No matter what route you take, you need to identify what problem you're trying to solve before you implement a different tool—whether it's a new CRM, Zapier integration, AI, website functionality or any other technology. You don't just want to bring on something else to manage.

Why Investors Love HALO

To some extent, **REVENUE** is always going to be a pain point—but it's not necessarily going to be your priority. There are a few occasions when it's more likely than others, such as startups and seed companies. With a two- or three-month runway in many cases, this can be a situation in which, "If we don't sell, we don't survive." Typically, the focus for such businesses would be on R's such as **RECOGNITION**, **RELATIONSHIPS**, and **REVENUE**, not so much **RECRUITMENT**, **REPUTATION**, or **RETENTION**. By its nature, a startup is more fragile, and any wrong decision hurts much more and more quickly.

In fact, one of my favorite success stories was a startup company that was getting pressured on their revenues by the angel investors who had provided outside funding. By implementing HALO, this company increased their efficiency and decreased their burn rate by so much that they extended their runway from six months to nine months. They had more control and clarity, could plan more accurately about what business to go after, and could disperse capital where it would deliver the best ROI.

The investors, who are accustomed to high burn rates, were stunned—and pleased—that their capital was going 50% farther. It also positioned the company perfectly for their B series financing.

What's the True Cost of a Meeting?

As noted above, HALO takes a wider perspective on **REVENUE** than just the money dropping into your accounts receivable department. When you don't control your expenses, it doesn't just decrease your profitability—it's an opportunity cost too. Every single dollar you waste is a dollar that can't be reinvested in your business, yet talking about expenses always seems to take a back seat. I'll give you two examples to underscore the point.

I was working with the owner of a creative marketing agency who was always complaining about his **REVENUE**—he'd been in the red for a few months and was having difficulty securing more clients. One day, I popped in to visit and saw a bunch of empty offices and cubicles. He'd shut down his entire company to do an all-day photoshoot of his people so they could update their website.

Instead of scheduling it out, having a few people come each hour, he literally had everyone sitting around all day.

You know me well enough by now to know what happened next. I asked, "Do you know how much this is costing you?"

"Well," he said, "the photographer's day rate is $3,000, which doesn't seem too bad, does it?"

I shook my head. "The problem isn't the photographer's fee," I said. "I mean how much are you paying everyone who's sitting around?"

When we ran the numbers, he had spent almost $10,000 to get a couple of dozen photos shot for his website. That was $10,000 that he surely could have spent in ways that drove revenues more directly.

Mind you, that was a special occasion—a company wasting a bunch of money on one day. I had another client that was particularly fond of meetings and committees, and I sometimes wondered if their employees did anything else. I took the CEO aside before their quarterly all-day meeting with the entire executive and leadership team, including several members who had to travel across the country to attend.

"Bill, give me a ballpark on what you think that meeting will cost," I said. He just shrugged his shoulders and said, "Hmm. I'm not sure."

So we broke out the scratch pad and this is what it looked like:

- *AVERAGE SALARY OF ATTENDEES: $250,000*
- *EXECUTIVES + LEADERS IN ATTENDANCE: 14*
- *MEETING COST FOR 4 HOURS: $6,720*
- *TRAVEL + LODGING PER QUARTER: $32,000*
- *QUARTERLY MEETING COST PER YEAR:* **$154,880.00**

I still remember the look of shock on Bill's face, because he'd never run the numbers. They were spending well over $150,000 a year for that quarterly meeting alone—and believe me, that was not the only time they got together.

Now, you may be thinking "That's a big company—we're much smaller and more efficient." Even if it's not an executive meeting among a bunch of highest-salaried leaders, the costs add up in the course of day-to-day business. Statistics show that the average employee in the US spends 31 hours a month in meetings, and 50% are a waste of time.[15] So let's run those numbers for a midsize company. (You might want to put away all sharp objects.)

- *AVERAGE SALARY OF ATTENDEES: $40/HOUR*
- *WASTED MEETING TIME: 15.5 HOURS/MONTH*
- *COST PER TEAM MEMBER: $620/MONTH*
- *TEAM MEMBERS: 8*
- *TOTAL COST OF MEETINGS PER MONTH: $4,960*
- *TOTAL COST OF MEETINGS PER YEAR:* **$59,520.00**

Before you schedule your next meeting, shine the HALO light in those dark corners. Ask yourself: What is our return on that investment? Is there a more effective way to get things done?

I'm not saying that you shouldn't have meetings, or that you could run a company without them. But it is a cautionary note that everything comes with a cost, and you can boost your profits by making it an objective to reduce wasted resources.

If you've ever said to yourself. . .

- *I can't afford to invest in marketing to build RECOGNITION. . .*
- *I can't hire a salesperson or pay my sales team more. . .*

---

15   These are just two of the statistics that illustrate how time is wasted in meetings. For 28 more of them, head to https://www.goldenstepsaba.com/resources/time-wasted-in-meetings

- *I don't have enough money to spend on RECRUITMENT or RETENTION...*

... it might be because you're burning capital in places that you don't even pay attention to. Just like your average person talks about spending more than they make, it's the same hazard in business—and then they wonder why they don't have any money.

GETTING TO THE POINT WHERE REVENUE TAKES CARE OF ITSELF

In the early stages of developing HALO, I would consistently hear entrepreneurs and executives confidently asserting that their pain was REVENUE. They would come up with ideas and strategies related to driving more income, frequently as a short-term initiative and other times with some lofty number in mind. I had more than a few people say they wanted to go from $1 million to $20 million in five years, or similar parabolic trajectories.

My goal was to help them understand that, more often than not, REVENUE would be a result of the efforts—not the destination. Pie-in-the-sky estimates can lead to spending money based on fictitious revenue numbers in your head, not reality. That can be a difficult thing to grapple with in the beginning, but if you build the other five R's using clear, actionable, and measurable strategies, the REVENUE will take care of itself. Thinking in smaller pieces—"We want to build strong RELATIONSHIPS in these specific geographic markets so we can sell XYZ product to these specific customers"—is the best way to accomplish that, not just setting a target out in the distance and blasting away at it.

With that, we've wrapped up our analysis of the 6R's. In the next section, we'll formulate your plan to activate them in your business.

To download a fillable PDF version of the exercises
in this chapter, visit *haloforall.com/hrh*

Six Key Takeaways

1. **REVENUE** happens when you build the other R's. It's the result of how everything else happens, not the destination.

2. Data is critical for understanding efficiency, making decisions, and understanding what's going to move the needle.

3. By focusing on the 6R's, you can make sure **REVENUE** peaks and valleys are not as dramatic.

4. There are only three ways to increase **REVENUE:** charge more, bring on more customers, or decrease expenses.

5. The integrated business cycle can help you squeeze more earnings out of **REVENUE** by doing more with less.

6. Expenses matter. Every single dollar you waste is a dollar that can't be reinvested in your business.

STEP 3:
EXECUTE

"Without execution, 'vision' is just another word for hallucination."

—Mark V. Hurd

EXECUTE:
ACTIVATE YOUR PLAN

Integrating the HALO building blocks to reach your vision of success.

The HALO framework is built around integrating the marketing, business development and sales, operations, human resources, customer service, and finance components of your business. When you break down the silos and replace them with a holistic model, you can clearly see the **RELATIONSHIPS** between each of the R's—and most important of all, you can harness the energy they create together. Once you generate enough energy through interconnectivity, it creates a halo effect—a ring of light in which strategy is tied to execution and everyone is working in collaboration.

And as you do, the progression looks like this:

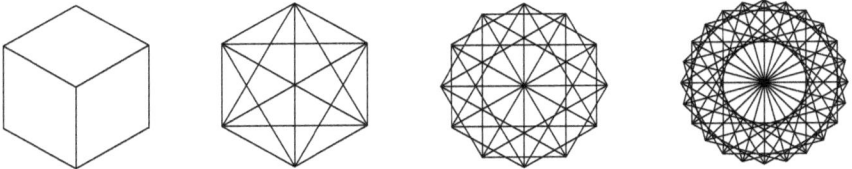

The ancillary effect of all that energy—and the protective halo it generates around your business—is that it actually allows you to slow down and think. You have more clarity and better focus. You're not as overwhelmed and your performance starts to improve. Maybe you don't even have to work quite so many hours, and you make better decisions because you have the time to be reflective instead of reactive. Bonus: Evolution actually leads to revolution (but don't tell your competition).

To this point, the work you've done and the exercises you've performed have been creating a foundation: understanding yourself, your company, the audiences you interact with, and where you stand on each of the 6R's, including pain points, obstacles, and opportunities. The HALO Execute process is where we assemble those building blocks and get the energy vortex spinning. Here's what to expect during this third step in the HALO process:

- **Prioritizing your R's:** In the past few chapters, you've been plugging your pain scale numbers into the chart on page 179— and now it's time to assess which of those you want to address as a priority. As a reminder to smaller organizations, you don't have to do all six, and while HALO clients generally take on three, you can do just one or two.

- **Setting your strategy:** Next, we'll set high-level strategic objectives for each one of the R's, while recognizing that not all of them will be immediate priorities. Part of this process will include a discussion of a value stick: How do we increase value to our external and internal audiences while maintaining profitability?

- **Tackling your tactics:** Next, we'll identify what actions and tactics are needed to reach each strategic objective. (Good news—you've already done a lot of the groundwork here in the Obstacles and Opportunities exercises in the 6R's chapters to direct those actions and tactics.)

- **Assigning accountability:** Time is our most precious resource, which means that it's ultra-important to delegate. While you might be the owner of a given strategic objective, you can't possibly do everything by yourself even if you wanted to—so who are the contributors on the tactical level?

- **Defining metrics and measurements:** Clarity around your strategic objectives is only part of the equation—you also need to track and measure the efficacy of your efforts or individuals that you hire. We'll discuss how you build metrics around each one of your R's, whether they are numbers, dollars, or percentages.

- **Creating your Avenues Plans**: The final piece of the HALO framework is to create your Avenues Plans, which will navigate your pathway to your future vision of success. Essentially, you'll be tying together the strategic objectives, tactics, accountability, and results into a cohesive plan for each of your prioritized R's.

Throughout the process, I'll provide real-life examples to help guide your understanding of how to approach the Execute process and exercises that will facilitate the creation of your own version of the plan. By the end, you'll have a clear path forward—and to ensure that your HALO program delivers maximum ROI for your business, I will offer some best-practices suggestions on how to keep your program on track during the next few months, years, and beyond.

"Most of us spend too much time on what is urgent and not enough time on what is important."

— STEPHEN COVEY

CHAPTER 10

PRIORITIZING YOUR R'S

The HALO pain scale tells us where to pay attention—and where we need to focus our strategic and tactical efforts.

If you've arrived at this chapter to fill in the pain scale of one of the 6R's, here's what you were looking for. Add the number in the appropriate space, and then head back to the chapter you were working on. We'll see you back here when you've completed all six!

RELATIONSHIPS

RECOGNITION

REPUTATION

PRIORITIES

01.

02.

03.

REVENUE

RECRUITMENT

RETENTION

If you're here because you've completed all six of the R's, congratulations. It's a significant task—and an important foundation for the Execute process—to define where you stand within the six problems and pain points that affect every single business on Earth.

At this point, with the chart complete, you may have a better understanding of why I recommended that you go into the exercises with an open mind, and without guessing or assuming what pain levels your team would identify. Our internal teams and the individuals on them may have different perceptions from us as leaders. We tell ourselves stories about why things are happening, but we may not have all the facts. While each individual's pain point assessment is technically subjective, the act of numerically defining and grouping additional opinions puts you on the road to being more objective.

In the beta-testing days, when we were implementing HALO at several clients and within our own office, we tried tackling all 6R's at once.

It wasn't impossible, but I'll be honest, it was overwhelming. Too many items to focus on, and not enough specific attention to the areas that needed it most, so it was fragmenting our efforts and diluting our efficacy.

Within a year, my team and I had reworked the methodology to better reflect what HALO was designed to accomplish in the first place: to enable clarity and alignment, allowing organizations to conserve resources and prevent burnout among teams and employees. We created a system to prioritize the R's that were going to make the most difference—and as a side benefit, it made it easier for clients to experience progress. When your team feels like something is working, there's a lot less resistance to a new way of doing things.

The reason I'm giving you that peek behind the HALO curtain is because I want you to make the process your own. There's no right or wrong answer, only the answers that work or don't for your individual circumstance. I do not recommend trying to address all 6R's at once, but if you have the time, resources, and chutzpah to pull it off, that is up to you.

DEFINING YOUR PRIORITY R'S AND MAINTENANCE R'S

Now that we've talked about what *not* to do, let's outline the current HALO best practices.

As human beings, pain tells us where to pay attention. The pain scale exercises in each of the R chapters are designed to do the same thing.

Think about the last time you had simultaneous injuries. For me, it was when I had a throbbing toothache on the same day that I'd twisted my ankle playing basketball, and my back was sore from horsing around with our kids. I needed to take care of the tooth first, because it was bad enough that I could barely hear myself think. I also knew that it was only going to get worse if I didn't deal with it.

The same is true in business: You need to take care of what is ailing you most or it could evolve into something even more painful.

These are your **PRIORITY R'S**. We're not going to overcomplicate this process, and there's no need to make it worse than a root canal. For example: If you've completed the chart at the top of this chapter and **RECOGNITION** is a 9, **REPUTATION** is an 8, and **RETENTION** is a 7—while everything else is a 5 or less—your path is pretty clear. Those are the priorities you should attack first. In the vast majority of cases, we encourage HALO practitioners to select no more than three to be the Priority R's.

In the event that you have high pain scales on four or more of the R's, the best way to choose your priorities will be to review them in light of the results from your obstacles and opportunities exercises. Talk with your team about where you think the most internal and external value can be created.

HALO is all about creating a holistic framework, so we're also going to address the remaining R's. These are your **MAINTENANCE R'S**. We will set a high-level strategy for them, because you still want clarity in terms of where you are today and what's the long-term vision of where you want to be.

Don't be surprised if you get a few weeks into the Execute process and find that you want to reorder your priorities. Sometimes you have to go beyond the pain point to discover the root problem. In particular, this tends to happen with companies that believe **REVENUE** is one of their top pain points. When they start to dive deeper into the tactics, strategies, and metrics, they often discover that it's really a matter of poor **RECRUITMENT:** for example, people who are lousy at their jobs hurting operations and creating a poor **REPUTATION**.

Keep in mind, these numbers aren't a blunt instrument, and you don't have to blindly go with the highest pain score. It's going to be about overcoming your obstacles and seizing your opportunities.

The end goal of the selection and prioritization process is to create harmony and balance at 30,000 feet. If you or your team start noticing a pain increase in one of the R's, you'll be able to diagnose it and treat it before it gets worse.

THE VALUE OF CREATING CLARITY

We live in a society of instant gratification, but that doesn't work in business. You need to play the long game. You need to be sustainable. It's like the old saying: The only reason you're sitting in the shade right now is because someone had the foresight to plant a tree 20 years ago.

The truth is, many companies succeed despite themselves, rushing to **REVENUE** rather than cultivating all of the 6R's. They manage to deliver services and sell products profitably without having explicit processes, consistency, or metrics to measure progress or identify shortcomings. Eventually their growth will hit a plateau, slam into a wall, or fall off a cliff. Knowing the pain scales of your 6R's, and thoughtfully prioritizing them, is a critical step in becoming more efficient and effective and growing sustainably.

Most important, having clarity around your pain points—both the priority and maintenance versions—gives you a starting point for creating actions and accountabilities to assign to the people in your group. In the next chapter, we'll talk about strategies and tactics to accomplish that.

Six Key Takeaways

1. Putting numbers on your pain points helps you move from subjectivity to objectivity.

2. Don't overcomplicate it.

3. Defining priority R's allows you to put resources where they're needed most.

4. Creating high-level strategy for maintenance R's ensures a holistic approach.

5. You may find that your priorities change as you start to formulate strategies and tactics—and that's OK!

6. Over the long haul, having clarity about pain points enables you to be more efficient and effective.

"**Strategy without tactics is the slowest route to victory. Tactics without strategy is the noise before defeat.**"

—SUN TZU

CHAPTER 11

Strategy, Tactics, and Accountability

What's going to add value, what steps are needed, and
who's going to get us to our strategic objective?

Among all the businesses that sound enjoyable but have the most cutthroat
competition, wineries surely rank near the top. While Illinois might not be Napa
or Sonoma when it comes to the number of grapes smashed annually, one of
our HALO clients was trying to distinguish themselves from the other 15 or so
wineries on their particular trail.

Most of the time, visitors would randomly stop at a few places on the route, but
the winery wanted to improve the number of people who specifically would
seek out their spot over the others—and who also would pay a higher dollar
amount for their products and services.

In other words, they needed a strategy. Based on their persona work, they
had identified two different customer tracks. The first group were those who
cared more about being entertained than the wines and the second set were
wine connoisseurs. For the former, it could be as simple as offering more live
entertainment on additional days of the week and doing promotions to drive

more local traffic. For the more discerning audiences—knowledgeable consumers who are really focused on the nuances of wine and processes—the strategy required skewing more towards exclusive vineyard tours and encouraging patrons to try the restaurant's wine flights and tasting menus that would appeal to the more sophisticated palate.

The common thread between the two? No matter the target customer, the vineyard needed to create more value to attract them.

THE SIMPLEST DEFINITION OF STRATEGY YOU'LL EVER SEE

Strategy is one of the foundational principles of HALO, since everything depends on creating alignment between our strategy and execution.

We want to be clear, efficient, and effective with our resources. That's true whether it's our personal time, or the time dedicated by our employees and partners whose talents we're leveraging. And it's certainly true about the dollars we're putting into growing our businesses, whether in marketing, business development, human resources or anything else. If we want to protect all of that, we need to align strategy and execution. Execution, as you may recall, is about the tactics—and that's the most familiar ground for many of us—but without a strategy to apply tactics towards, you're just checking tasks off a list.

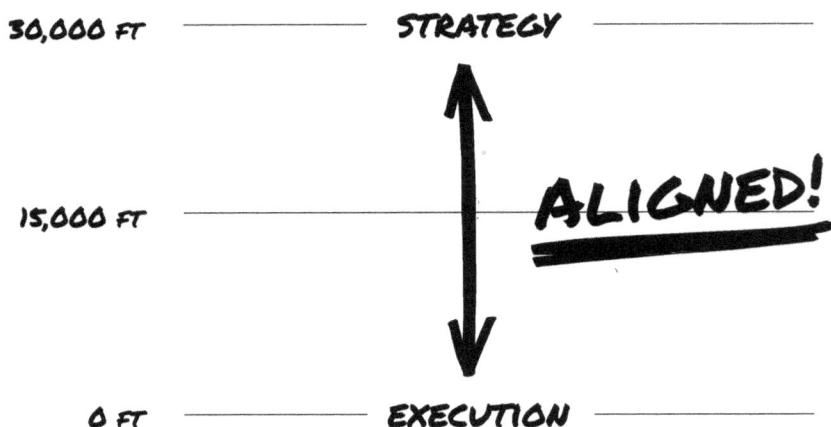

30,000 FT	——— STRATEGY ———
15,000 FT	——————↑———— ALIGNED!
0 FT	——— ↓ EXECUTION ———

Whenever I start working with an organization—in front of large groups or just a few individuals—I often kick things off by asking "What is strategy?"

As you can imagine, the flurry of answers is all over the place. "It's a tool!" "It's an idea!" "It's a plan!"

One time, I had a guy scream at me, "That's your job to tell us!" I may not have agreed with his approach, but he wasn't wrong. So let's give it a shot.

Strategy is a way of creating more value for our external and internal audiences.

But let's break this down a little bit, and reframe the concept into something you can ask yourself or your team.

STRATEGY

"HOW DO WE CREATE MORE VALUE FOR _____ ?"

(PROSPECTS, PARTNERS, CUSTOMERS, EMPLOYEES...)

Whatever your audience is, your strategy is going to revolve around answering this question.

UNDERSTANDING THE VALUE STICK

The general concept of a value stick was originally developed by Harvard Business School professor Felix Oberholzer-Gee.[16] In a HALO context, it's represented as a tall I-shaped bar with your external audiences at the top, such as prospects,

---

16   "Better, Simpler Strategy: A Value-Based Guide to Exceptional Performance," https://www.amazon.com/Better-Simpler-Strategy-Value-Based-Exceptional/dp/1633699692

customers, or partners. On the bottom of the I, we have our internal audiences that are working within our boundaries—in other words front-line employees, managers, executives, etc.

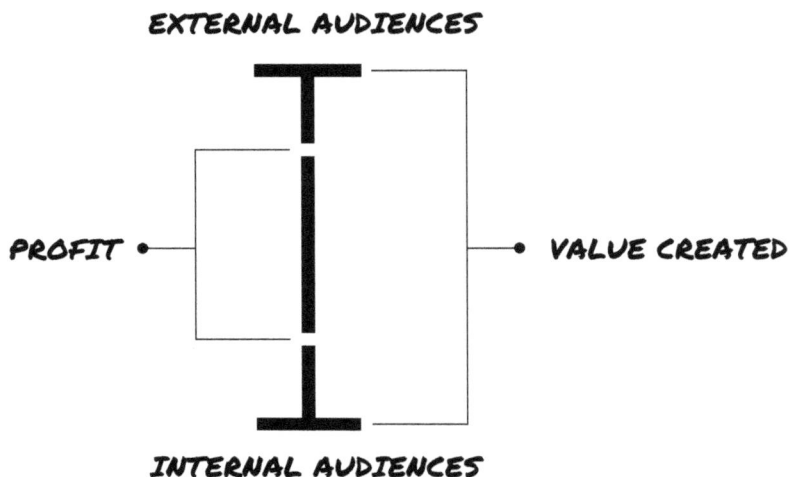

EXTERNAL AUDIENCES

PROFIT •   • **VALUE CREATED**

INTERNAL AUDIENCES

Between those two ends of the I is where we create our value. That could be through our products and services for external audiences, or a superior working environment for our internal teams.

Finally, the point in the middle is where you're getting your profit from—and it will fluctuate, depending on how efficient and effective you are. Stretching that section requires increasing the value to external and internal audiences:

- How do we encourage an external audience to buy from us, maintain a relationship with us, and eventually promote us?

- In our hiring processes, what are the compensation, benefits, and quality of life elements that are going to enable us to recruit and retain talent?

Answering those questions is going to define not only the top-line strategy but the tactics you are going to execute. Let's solidify these concepts with some exercises.

EXERCISE #1   Developing Your Strategic Objectives

Our strategic objectives are the desired outcomes.

- *They drive the data we want and need to collect.*

- *They drive decisions in whatever we want to do and where we want to go.*

- *They drive discipline in where we are focusing and provide clarity in what we're trying to accomplish—including what we communicate to contributors and partners.*

Strategic objectives are essential enough to business success that we will create them around each one of our R's, regardless of the priority.

The strategic objective formula is as follows:

(Build/Increase) (one of the 6R's) for (brand/product) as (value position) with (audience/funnel) in (market/region/geography).

As you can see, the structure of that formula correlates phrases with work you've already completed in your anatomy, audience, and vision of success.

For example, here's what some good strategic objectives would look like for a B2B HR and benefits company called Wholesome in Southern California:

- *Build RECOGNITION with prospects for Wholesome as the premier brand for employee benefits, HR, and retirement offerings in Los Angeles and San Diego to drive engagement, marketing qualified leads (MQLs), and sales qualified leads (SQLs).*

- *Build RELATIONSHIPS with clients and community and industry partners for Wholesome in Los Angeles and San Diego to drive $5 million in revenue.*

- *Build Wholesome's REPUTATION as the premier brand for employee benefits, HR, and retirement through operations, service delivery, and adherence to core values with prospects, clients, and partners in Los Angeles and San Diego to drive $5 million in revenue.*

- **RECRUIT** the right talent for Wholesome that aligns with our anatomy for open positions in Los Angeles and San Diego to serve our employee benefits, HR, and retirement clients.

- **RETAIN** highly engaged and enthusiastic clients at Wholesome who align with our anatomy in Los Angeles and San Diego.

- Increase top-line **REVENUE** to $5 million and bottom-line profitability to 20% for Wholesome in Los Angeles and San Diego.

I'm not going to overcomplicate this exercise—and you shouldn't either. Using that formula and those examples, create one or two strategic objectives for each of your 6R's. It's an important foundation that is going to lead to your development and use of data. It's going to enhance your ability to make insightful and analytical decisions, rather than anecdotal ones. And it's going to drive discipline for yourself and for those who are helping you.

Like the shampoo bottle says, rinse and repeat for each of the 6R's.

EXERCISE #2 Tackling Tactics

Tactics are the steps, actions, and processes that are going to help us move down the path to reach our strategic objective—the 15,000 to zero range. Like strategy, tactics can also be easily understood in the form of a question:

What specific steps are needed to reach the strategic objective?

I'm here to bring you some good news: If you've completed the "Obstacles and Opportunities" exercises in each of the 6R chapters, you've already done the heavy lifting here. You can use what you've already brainstormed and documented to direct your actions and tactics going forward.

Tactics not only align with the strategic objective, but define the actions and steps needed to execute. In the process, most companies will find gaps—and that's OK! Sometimes a system or process will need to be created. When it comes to effectiveness and efficiency, automation is one of the most common opportunities: repetitive steps that can be systemized can be made increasingly faster. Even if you can't implement something right now, seeing the pattern can alert you to its future potential.

Here's an example of a tactics list, using a company whose strategic objective is "Build **RECOGNITION** for Acme Marketing services with prospects and partners in the Pacific Northwest":

- ☑ **RESEARCH PR OPPORTUNITIES IN SEATTLE, PORTLAND, SPOKANE, AND BOISE**
- ☑ **RESEARCH TRADE SHOWS IN THOSE CITIES**
- ☑ **FIND MARKETING PARTNER**
- ☑ **RESEARCH SEO KEYWORDS**
- ☑ **CREATE CONTENT CALENDAR**
- ☑ **REVIEW MARKETING BUDGET**
- ☑ **BRAINSTORM LEAD MAGNETS**
- ☑ **CREATE VIDEO TESTIMONIALS**

Don't let that list limit you—tactics can be just about anything you dream up:

- ☑ **EDUCATIONAL TOOLS**
- ☑ **BOOKS OR EXCERPTS**
- ☑ **COUPONS**
- ☑ **HOW-TO VIDEOS**
- ☑ **VIP PRIVILEGES**
- ☑ **SPECIAL EVENTS**

Basically, a tactic needs to add value and give you an edge when someone is choosing between your product or service and someone else's.

EXERCISE #3 **Assign Champions and Contributors**

When we're thinking about accountability within HALO, we split the concept between champions and contributors. It's just as it sounds: The champion is the person responsible for the strategic objective itself, where the buck stops, the person who everyone else reports to. Contributors are those who are helping execute the tactics, the foot soldiers helping achieve the strategic objectives under the direction of the champion.

In this exercise, we need to ask: "Who will get us to our strategic objective?"

While there is only one internal champion, there can be multiple contributors depending on the size and complexity of a tactic. A marketing project, for example, might include the person in charge of your website, a graphic designer, a copywriter, and your social media manager—and don't forget the salesperson who's going to receive the leads that are generated. It's a team effort, with the leader being clear about what needs to be accomplished and the individual contributors building out their tactical components as needed.

For those of you running smaller businesses, I can hear you. "But Rob, we're tiny. We don't have a robust team." Yeah, I get it. But the act of creating standards and practices is going to help you in the long run as you build out your team. It's a healthier and more mature business mindset. Any step you can take to-wards being more efficient and effective is a step away from being overworked, overwhelmed, and underperforming.

I know because I've lived it. Biting off more than I can chew, resisting delegation because it seemed easier to do it myself than trying to explain.

Sure, I'll let us off the hook a little. It's not necessarily because we're control freaks (although some of us are). It's because the business is our baby. We've put everything we have into it.

But one of my favorite comments from a HALO client was when I pulled her aside about six months into the process and asked her how it was going.

"Everything is amazing," she said. "My team finally knows what to do and what they're accountable for, and they do exactly what I need them to do. Now I have time to work on the business, not in the business."

That was my goal for her, and it's my goal for you too. Let your strategic objective champions and contributors work in the business while you focus on growing—and creating more value externally, internally, and for yourself.

REVENUE happens when you loosen the reins a bit.

WILLPOWER AND FOLLOW-THROUGH

If you're my age, you remember the *Karate Kid* movies—and if you're younger, you've probably seen the modern *Cobra Kai* TV series. The exercises that the aspiring karate champions participate in aren't particularly exciting. Wax on, wax off. Paint up, paint down. It was painful and time-consuming, and then in the end, the kids can defend themselves and reach their potential.

A few years ago, my wife and I started going to a fantastic personal trainer. He's not cheap, but he's worth every dime if you put in the effort. Well, my wife did, and I didn't. So she got fit and I didn't.

It had nothing to do with the program or the exercises, and everything to do with my willpower and my follow through. In addition to seeing him once or twice a week, he also expects you to work out three more times and to eat according to the plan. I didn't do either.

HALO is a lot of things, but it's not a magic wand. It only works if you do. You're going to need to push through some dead ends and learn what doesn't work. But in the a-ha moments, when you find the things that do work, the efficiency, effectiveness, and growth potential are incredible.

Six Key Takeaways

1. Strategy is a way of creating more value for our external and internal audiences.

2. Strategic objectives are the desired outcomes.

3. Tactics answer the question: "What specific steps are needed to reach the strategic objective?"

4. Champions and contributors answer the question: "Who will get us to our strategic objective?"

5. Let your strategic objective champions and contributors work in the business while you focus on growing.

6. Willpower and follow through are essential for reaching your potential.

"If the metrics you are looking at aren't useful in optimizing your strategy — stop looking at them."

— Mark Twain

CHAPTER 12

METRICS, MEASUREMENTS, AND AVENUES

Harnessing strategic objectives, tactics, data, and
accountability to determine your future path

At the time we started out with one of our industrial HALO clients, they were a
seasoned company doing millions in annual revenue—by that measure, pretty
damn successful. Behind the curtain, however, they were struggling with a massive
amount of turnover among managers and employees—as much as 40% in one
year alone. This turnover was symptomatic of much deeper issues. No vision.
No clear objectives or ways to measure them. Zero accountability. Same old
story: Overworked, overwhelmed, and underperforming. It was a low-morale
culture, with more finger pointing than high fiving.

I have a vivid memory of the first day I started working with this client, sitting in
the break room, just having a casual chat with the new CEO over a cup of coffee.

"There are a lot of days that I have no idea what I'm supposed to be doing," he
said. "And I also don't know what I'm supposed to do about it."

His words were like a gut punch. I've felt that sense of frustration and helplessness before. My guess is, you have too. It's like you're stuck in a disorienting maze of your own making and you can see a map that might help you find a way out, but it's never within arm's reach. And the hardest part is that, deep down, you know you could figure out what you're supposed to be doing—if only you could see the bigger picture, the whole map of how you got here, where you desire to go, and what's stopping you from getting there.

One of the biggest challenges for this company was their lack of strategy to execution. We went through all the same steps and exercises that you've gone through: anatomy, audiences, the 6R's. They set their objectives, tactics, and accountability. And they reached the point on the HALO journey that you're at right now: *How do we measure success?*

Whenever we start a HALO engagement with an established company, they almost always believe that they know how to track and measure their performance. Within the first 90 days, we task them with formulating their metrics and data and ask them to report back. Without fail, a majority come back to the table and admit, "Yeah, actually, we don't know how to do this correctly."

They recognize how important it is to track their key results, but when they put pen to paper, they realize that they're behind the eight ball when it comes to business intelligence and data analytics. Almost everyone knows how to track revenue and profitability, but when it comes to cost to acquire, return on your marketing investment, churn rate, cost of turnover, and so on? Not so much. It's a bridge that many businesses don't know how to cross, or they might not even know where the bridge is located. In many cases, they don't even have the lumber, concrete, or nuts and bolts to build it.

METRICS AND MEASUREMENT

I've written a lot in general about metrics and measurement in this book, and that's where we're going to focus first. We're in a data-driven world, and in HALO, data is what will drive your strategy and tactics into the future.

While metrics and measurement often get treated as equivalent, there's a subtle distinction to be made. Metrics are quantifiable measures used to track, monitor, and assess the status or performance of specific aspects of an organization, project, or process—such as sales lead conversion, customer satisfaction, or employee retention. They're used for comparative and analytical purposes; when tied to strategic objectives, they can be used to drive improvements and help you focus on what matters most.

Measurements are the actual data or values that you obtain, whether raw numbers or observations. They aren't necessarily tied to business objectives, but become meaningful when used to calculate metrics. For example, the number of website visitors and conversions are measurements, which can be used to calculate conversion rate, a metric.

If you're wondering why I've waited till the end to talk in detail about metrics and measurement, it's because it's too easy to get bogged down in the data: *How do I gather it and track it? Do I even know which metrics matter most? What's the difference between measurements and metrics, again? HELP ME!* By waiting until the execution phase, we can leverage the momentum you've already established to tackle these questions effectively. The metrics you choose to measure today are critical for determining your future successes.

If you've been in the business world for more than a minute, you'll recognize this famous quote:

> *"What gets measured, gets managed."*
> —PETER DRUCKER

We need to be able to manage with clarity so we can make decisions that are actually actionable—and the only way to do that is to start measuring against your strategic objectives. By focusing on specific key results, we can reach our desired outcomes. Metrics and measurements help us connect our strategies from start to finish, making our processes efficient and effective all the way through our execution. Most of the biggest problems companies face, like the one I mentioned earlier, happen because there's a gap between the big-picture strategy and the day-to-day actions. It's vital to measure and manage every step of the way, from the broad strategy at 30,000 feet down to the smallest details at 0 feet.

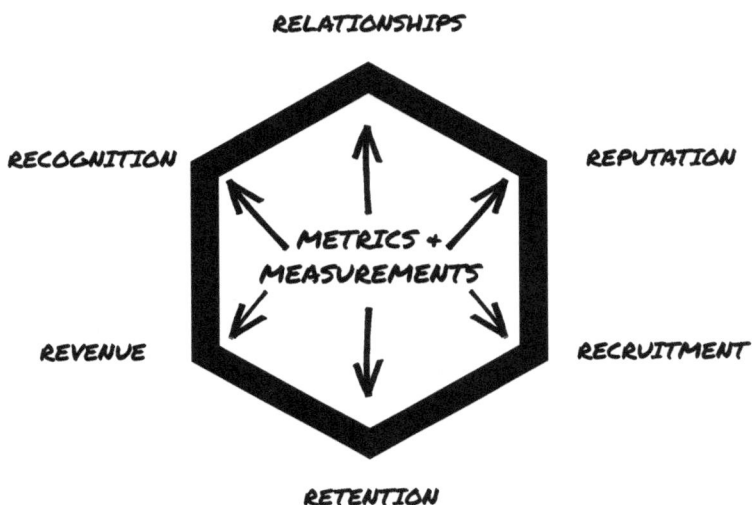

You can think of metrics like the dashboard in your car. While **REVENUE** serves as the speedometer, there's a whole lot more that tells you how an engine is running—or if it's showing signs of trouble. RPMs, oil and radiator temperatures, how much fuel you've got in the tank (or how much charge you've got left in the ol' EV)—and even cabin temperature so that you can dial in your comfort.

In my advertising days, I'd meet with new prospects and clients, and most of the time they were dissatisfied with their previous agency relationship. (That's why they were meeting with me.) But when I asked them, "How did you measure the agency that came before us?" the response was inevitably the same: either a blank stare or "**REVENUE**."

At the risk of defending my former competitors, that's a losing situation from day 1. If there aren't clear and actionable metrics, how the heck are you supposed to prove your value? To extend the car metaphor, what would happen if your car just had a speedometer and no check-engine light or gauges on the dashboard?

You'd be fine. . . until you were broken down on the side of the road.

Metrics should be built around each one of your 6R's—with the caveat that it's most essential for your priority R's when you're getting started. Within our various HALO clients, we've accumulated well over 400 different data points that have business utility, and we're adding new ones all the time.

Here's a quick "greatest hits" list of metrics for each of the R's:

RECOGNITION (MARKETING)

- *Website traffic (#,%)*
- *Social media metrics (#,$,%)*
- *Brand awareness surveys (#,%)*
- *Search volume data (#,%)*
- *Impressions (#,%)*
- *Click-through rate (CTR) (#,%)*
- *Media coverage (#)*
- *Net promoter score (NPS) (#)*
- *Customer acquisition cost (CAC) ($,%)*

RELATIONSHIPS (BUSINESS DEVELOPMENT)

- *Marketing qualified leads (MQL) (#,%)*
- *Sales qualified leads (SQL) (#,%)*
- *Conversion rate (MQL to SQL) (#,%)*
- *Leads (#,%)*
- *Opportunities (#,%)*
- *Customers (#,%)*
- *Sales cycle length (#,%)*
- *Lead-to-customer conversion rate (#,%)*

- Customer acquisition cost (CAC) (#,$)
- Revenue ($)

Reputation (Operations)

- Customer satisfaction score (CSAT) (%)
- Net promoter score (NPS) (#)
- Employee satisfaction and turnover rate (%)
- Social media sentiment analysis (%)
- Product/service reviews (#,%)
- Customer retention rate (%)

Recruitment (Talent Acquisition)

- Time to hire (#)
- Cost per hire ($)
- Quality of hire (%)
- Offer acceptance rate (%)
- Applicant to interview ratio (#,%)
- Interview to offer ratio (#,%)
- Source of hire (#,%)
- Diversity of candidates (#,%)
- Employee referral rate (#,%)
- Job offer-to-acceptance ratio (%)
- Retention rate (%)

Retention (Customer)

- Customer retention rate (CRR) (#,%)
- Customer churn rate (#,%)

- *Customer lifetime value (CLV) ($,%)*
- *Net promoter score (NPS) (#)*
- *Repeat purchase rate (#,%)*
- *Purchase frequency (#,%)*
- *Average order value (AOV) ($,%)*
- *Customer profitability score ($,%)*
- *Customer engagement (#,%)*
- *Customer satisfaction score (CSAT) (#,%)*

REVENUE (FINANCE)

- *Customer retention rate (CRR): Revenue*
- *Gross profit margin ($,%)*
- *Net profit margin ($,%)*
- *Operating income ($,%)*
- *Operating expense ratio ($,%)*
- *Cash flow ($,%)*
- *Accounts receivable (AR) aging (#,$,%)*
- *Accounts payable (AP) aging (#,$,%)*
- *Return on investment (ROI) ($,%)*
- *Working capital ($,%)*
- *Debt-to-equity ratio ($,%)*

Keep in mind, that's only a snapshot from several hundred options. Data can quickly become overwhelming, and that's the opposite of what we're trying to achieve. You need to give yourself the leeway to learn about data—and know in advance you're going to discover what doesn't work as well as what does, and it's going to take time to evolve.

Let's demonstrate with a simplified example, with the acknowledgement that this is a cross-country drive and not a drag race (but you'll be in a new car with an engine that's firing on all cylinders and all the gauges work). Take a startup internet retailer that has identified **RECOGNITION** as its biggest pain point. At the moment, they're a relatively unknown name in the market and trying to gain a foothold.

RECOGNITION

Strategic Objective: Build **RECOGNITION** for ABC SportsGear as the premier athletic clothing line with prospects in the Southeast.

Metrics	Measurement (#, $, %)	Benchmark	Goal
Website traffic	#	8,342 unique visits in Q3	14,000 unique visits in Q4
Conversion rate (completed sales per unique visit)	%	2% in Q3	3% in Q4
Customer acquisition cost	$	No data in Q3	$200 in Q4

I want to call your attention to a few aspects of the chart.

- Each of the measurements, benchmarks and goals has a number, dollar amount or percentage associated with it. Obviously, you could track any data point in any type of metric—for example, this company might want to track total customers, overall revenues, or revenue per customer—but there needs to be a reason for including it.

- You'll see that it's OK to have "no data" in any one of the fields. If you're just launching, the benchmarks may be all empty at first—and that's fine.

- Each of the data points is quarterly. Depending on your circumstance, that time period might be longer or shorter—but you should always have a time frame associated with the figure.

- Finally, the data points are specific. We don't just want visits; we want unique visits, because that tells us they're new visitors. We want conversions from unique visits, too, not just from people who've previously been on our site. Looking at their analytics, this company could drill down only on visits from people in their geographic area of the Southeast, since that's their target market.

Taken as a whole, these data points are going to tell the company whether their **RECOGNITION** actions and tactics are working. Above all, they will serve as a foundation for making data-driven decisions to guide future campaigns. In conjunction with knowing who's accountable, as far as champions and contributors, you'll also know who needs to follow through on what they're supposed to do.

Based on what revenue numbers this company is trying to hit, they will have a much better idea of how many marketing qualified leads and sales qualified leads they need in order to get there. Knowing the conversion rate will help drive consistent revenue and consistent profitability.

But again, it's not just about revenue and profit. They're trying to build a business much as trying to build a bank account.

Unless you are a very mature business with data collection that's already robust, less is more in the beginning. Don't go crazy with metrics. Focus on the top one to three categories that you think will be most influential for reaching your strategic objective.

Avenues Plan: A Pathway to Reaching Your Strategic Objectives

"The best way to predict the future is to create it."

—Peter Drucker

Along with your **Anatomy** and **Audiences**, **Avenues** are the third component in the core structure of HALO.

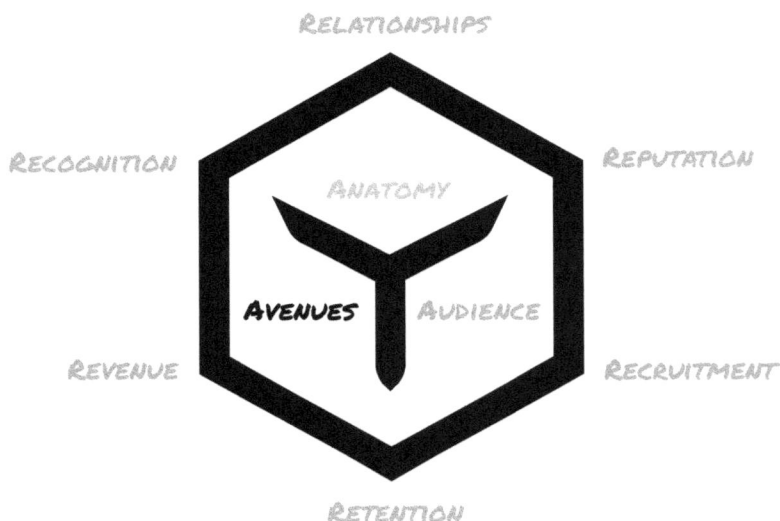

From the outset of this book, everything has revolved around resetting your vision of success. Where do you want to be in the future? How are you going to create it?

Avenues Plans can be thought of as pathways or roadmaps that meticulously map out the journey from a strategic objective to the subsequent measurement of its future success.

Avenues Plans serve as detailed guides outlining how to navigate from a defined goal towards its successful achievement, providing clarity and direction throughout the execution phase of any project or strategy, and encompassing all necessary actions and tactics that need to be executed.

Avenues Plans get us from point A, where we are today, to point B, our future state in three years or whatever time frame you have set. Unlike Google Maps, which I rely on whenever I go someplace new even if it's 10 minutes away, we're the only ones who can create our own routes.

This process is about seizing the opportunities that not only have the highest revenue potential, but that also offer the right fit for us. After all, HALO isn't about comparing ourselves to others. It's about finding the right path for each of us individually.

I realize that this book has been heavy on the exercises to this point. But here's your benefit: You're going to create your Avenues Plans based on all the work you've already done.

To assimilate your strategy and tactics and provide accountability, every single one of your 6R's will have an Avenues Plan associated with it, whether it's one of your priority R's or one of the maintenance R's. Every Avenues Plan follows this structure:

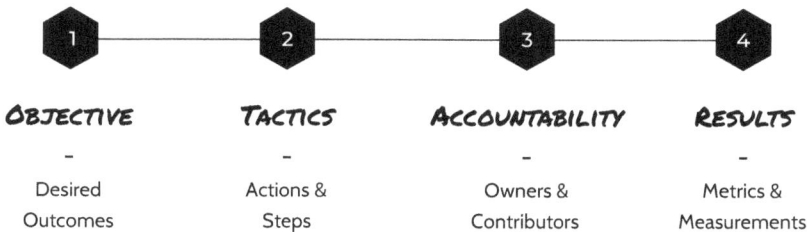

OBJECTIVE	*TACTICS*	*ACCOUNTABILITY*	*RESULTS*
–	–	–	–
Desired Outcomes	Actions & Steps	Owners & Contributors	Metrics & Measurements

Let's walk through an example:

First is the high-level strategic objective. "What do we want to achieve and over what time frame?"

Next are the tactics and action items. "What do we specifically need to do for the next 4 quarters to reach that objective?"

Then, you have accountability: "Who is the champion and who are the contributors?"

Finally, the results are the metrics by which you can define success. "What are the measurements, benchmarks, and goals that will get us where we want to go?"

The HALO framework is comprehensive, not complicated. It's up to you whether you want to work on all 6R's at once or just one. That may depend on other elements, such as whether you are doing it yourself or incorporating a larger executive team, or the timeline you have for your vision of success. Just remember that the HALO framework is all about harmony. Each of the 6R's works together like an instrument section in an orchestra, creating a symphony of success. You have the flexibility to decide whether you want to fine-tune all aspects or focus on one at a time. It's all about finding your rhythm. I can't hand you the sheet music for every detail, but that's the beauty of it. Ambiguity is more than OK, it's beneficial because that's where the real creativity comes from. So, use the ease and power of HALO to compose your own unique success story.

The goal is to participate in the process, understanding inputs, and co-creating together using a common language. This approach moves us away from the blame game and allows everyone to contribute freely. While Marketing will typically lead the **RECOGNITION** plan, their expertise doesn't overshadow input from other departments. By incorporating diverse perspectives, we're breaking down silos and boosting our collective effectiveness. When we embrace this collaborative approach, we make innovation our new norm.

The procedures below are based on best practices that we've developed in years of engaging with HALO clients—but they are not you, and you are not them. These are frameworks that contain the entire organizational structure; what you fill them with is up to you. Every aspect of HALO is about alignment, and that is more important than any single R. Your team members don't know what their coworkers are thinking and feeling until you give them an opportunity to talk about it.

I've seen HALO implemented successfully by entrepreneurs, division leaders, HR VPs, and chief marketing officers. I've seen a range of management styles, from autocratic to laissez-faire. Depending on your organizational structure and how big your company is, it might mean having several leaders being mixed and matched. It doesn't matter. The best advice I can give is asking "Who's most connected to all of the internal groups in our organization? Who can create the most harmony?"

The duration of your Avenues Plans will depend on the scope of the objective and the actions required to accomplish them—most often, that will be a quarter or a year. It will also depend on your company's maturity level. If you are at stage one, for example, you may be just creating the infrastructure for data collection, while a company with a sophisticated CRM is making decisions based on far more granular information.

INSTILLING ACCOUNTABILITY

Which brings us to the role of accountability, which applies to everyone in your organization—including you as the leader. The way HALO approaches accountability, however, isn't a traditional boss-driven hierarchy. It's designed to create a sense of ownership and responsibility among all employees, driving everyone—no matter where you sit on the org chart—to be more engaged, productive, and ultimately contribute to the success of the organization. In addition to harmony, transparency, clarity, and alignment, HALO is intended to create accountability from 30k to zero feet.

As a foundation for every Avenues Plan, you will create a document that states the plan for the next 12 months, along with a list of steps and people who are specifically responsible and the metrics against which they're being measured. And here's the key: *Every single champion and contributor signs the document.*

When you do a quarterly review, for example, it will be clear where each person stands in the chain of progress. If someone has only completed seven or 10 tasks, they can be held accountable. Ideally, using 30- and 60-day reviews, you can catch those items even earlier, because you're constantly monitoring and checking in.

Without clarity, alignment, and metrics, however, people can skirt accountability quickly. It's not enough to say "We're going to build **RECOGNITION** in the market." Does that mean 100 marketing qualified leads? Ten signups for a product? Fifty blog posts? It needs to be on a signed piece of paper.

Of course, accountability can occasionally mean a conversation about con-sequences—and this is never comfortable. An executive team who sees an uncompleted major task, after resources and budget have been allocated, probably needs a head to roll. Conversely, those on the ground dealing with micromanaging and/or changing expectations from leadership are empowered to speak up, too. You can't expect perfection, but doing nothing is not the right message either.

Identifying Your Avenues Plan Cadence

I've seen strategic systems and consultants that prescribe a meeting every week or two. But by now, you've seen my opinion on meetings and how much they cost if they start to multiply. Ultimately, it's up to leadership and the teams, but the best practice is to create a regular cadence (sample below) when the whole group is going to get back together and touch base. I recommend against meeting too frequently; it's preferable to let people be independent to the extent you can. Accountability is the point—you're seeing how much a team can accomplish while maintaining quality—and personal agency is a wonderful byproduct that keeps team members motivated and feeling satisfied about their work.

I recommend checking in on the progress within the various 30-day spans and offering your support where it's needed. Ideally, you want teams to be self-directed, but realistically that's not always going to be the case right out of the gate. You don't want to get to day 25 and discover no one's done anything. One way is to create a sub-plan that gives a reason to check in: "Within two weeks, you should have a basic outline developed. Send it to me and let's look at it together."

Sample Avenues Plan Timeline

Day 1: Assign accountability

- *Identify champion and contributors*
- *Discuss situation and objectives at high level*

DAY 30: CHECK-IN #1

- Avenues Plan outline due
- Define tactics/approach and results

DAY 60: CHECK-IN #2

- Full Avenues Plan ready for approval
- Acquire signatures from champion and all contributors

DAY 90: ACTIVATION

- Budgets and schedules approved
- Vendors selected
- Technologies purchased/in development
- Initiate measuring processes

Note, day 90 is also an important deadline for deciding the items you *don't* wish to focus on right now. Maybe you were unable to harvest certain data points, or you couldn't secure enough budget to tackle certain tasks. But this doesn't mean you're eliminating them from the overall plan! Instead, put them in a queue of "forward look" items for the next quarter or beyond.

DAY 180 AND 270: QUARTERLY CHECK-INS

You will be having team meetings as needed to keep on track with your Avenues Plan. The quarterly meetings are for two specific discussions :

1. What, if anything, can we add to our tracking and measurement in the following quarter? This discussion is about looking at the performance and deciding if we need to change, add, or delete any metrics and or measurements to get us closer to the objective. It's common that many teams will find the metrics and

or measurements they believed were good indicators of tracking toward the objective are NOT in fact the right ones.

2. Based on our performance in the current quarter, what actions do we need to take in the next quarter?

In other words, by the time we get to the next quarter, we're tracking and measuring our past results plus the results that we weren't able to get to previously. It's a process of refining and optimizing. Are we on track or off track? If we're off, what do we need to change that over the next quarter?

You're also going to find things that you thought were important to track and measure really aren't that important, or maybe impossible.

YEAR-END: ANNUAL ALIGNMENT

Having gone through the Avenues Plan process and subsequent three quarters of it being activated, it's time to review how you did.

- *What does the data tell us, as far as results vs. strategic objectives?*

- *What do we want to do in the following year? Is there a different R that has had a pain increase and that we need to prioritize? Is there an R that's now painless enough to put in the maintenance category?*

- *How does all of this align to our two- or three-year vision of success?*

From that point, you're always rolling forward on a 90-day cadence of planning, tracking, measuring, and augmenting. You're not waiting a year to plan the next year—which honestly makes life easier, since it's more a matter of updating and following a plan.

It sounds like a long way off, but I will note that, for most HALO companies, the start of year 3 is a good time to start evolving your next 3-year vision of success.

The ultimate point of Avenues Plans is to enable you to grow faster and with more predictability: a business that's fully in alignment, hiring people that fit (and getting rid of the bad apples), connecting with the right partners, and holding everyone accountable. As the leader, you know where you want to go. Equally important, you can clearly provide direction to your entire management team, filtering through the middle managers and all the way down to customer service reps and other front-line employees.

Everybody knows what they're supposed to do, and **REVENUE** is happening as a result.

I'll wrap up this chapter with a visual representation of HALO.

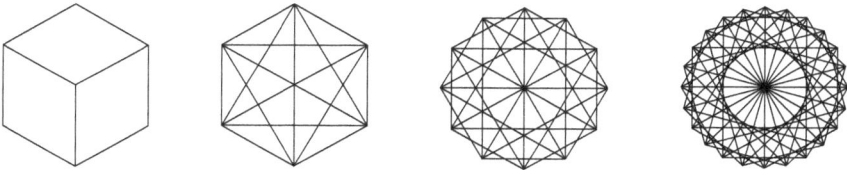

Starting from the left, we're setting our foundation, and step-by-step through the right, we're building momentum and creating a protective light around our business. You may be on the left side on stage one now, but take a moment to visualize what you're going to feel like once you've evolved into stage four: no longer overworked, overwhelmed, and underperforming, but instead operating at optimal efficiency and effectiveness.

SIX KEY TAKEAWAYS

1. In a data-driven world, metrics and measurements are what will drive your strategy and tactics into the future.

2. Never forget Peter Drucker's wise words: "What gets measured, gets managed."

3. At the same time, you don't need to go crazy with metrics—less is more in the beginning.

4. Avenues meticulously map out the journey from a strategic objective to the subsequent measurement of its success.

5. Avenues Plans are about finding the right path for each of us individually, so we can live our best lives and do our best work.

6. Identifying your cadence allows you to constantly refine and optimize your Avenues Plans and business evolution.

"Change is hard at first, messy in the middle, and so gorgeous at the end."

– Robin Sharma

CHAPTER 13

LETTER TO YOUR FUTURE SELF

When you hit the HALO wall, remind yourself
why you started the process in the first place.

Every client experiences a HALO honeymoon, a time when the processes are fresh, interesting, and energizing and the gains come easily and quickly. Maybe it's not quite like sitting in the shade of a palm tree with a piña colada in your hand, but the next best thing.

I'm here to tell you, however, there is also going to come a time—maybe in three months, six months, or a year—that you're going to be frustrated as heck. You've heard marathon runners talk about "the wall": a moment of overwhelming fatigue or excruciating pain that strikes a few miles before the finish. Similarly, the HALO wall might arrive in several forms: internal "is-this-really-worth-it" doubts in your own head as a leader, metrics that always seem just out of reach, or a minor rebellion amongst staff members who don't enjoy being accountable or are stuck in the way they've always done it.

But I'm telling you right now, it's going to happen—because I've seen it with every HALO client we've worked with. It's inherent in the nature of change.

It's uncomfortable. You're going to fail on some things. And I've been honest with you all the way along that it's going to be messy and hard before it gets gorgeous, right?

What I don't want, since you've come this far, is for you to give up.[17] The simplest way to push through the inevitable is to remind yourself of how you got here in the first place.

With that thought in mind, here's the exercise we use with HALO consulting clients.

1. Get out an envelope and write, in big, bold letters on the front:

OPEN WHEN I WANT TO QUIT

2. Grab a pad and pen or open a Word document and jot down a letter to your future self. This is obviously a very personal exercise, so I can't tell you exactly what to write, but consider answering some of the following questions as a prompt:

- *Why did you pick up a copy of* How Revenue Happens *(or why did one of your friends or colleagues believe it would be helpful to you)?*

- *What was the current state of your business the day before you started the HALO process?*

- *What was the status of each of your R's?*

- *What were your 3 to 6 biggest pain points?*

- *What were you hoping to achieve with the HALO program, and how long did you think it would take?*

- *Based on your current physical and emotional state, what do you want to tell your future self—especially knowing why you will be opening this letter?*

---

17   For some great insights on this topic, check out Seth Godin's *The Dip: A Little Book That Teaches You When to Quit (and When to Stick).*

3. Seal the envelope and put it somewhere you'll be able to find it when the critical moment arrives.

HALO is a crawl, walk, and run process. You are going to slip and fall along the way as you learn, adapt, and transform the way you operate your business. It's a big shift in how we work and why, and that's not always easy. I can give you the tools to push through and get to the other side, but your role is to remind yourself why you're doing this—and give yourself the forgiveness of not being perfect. If you keep going, and break the habits that are keeping you from succeeding, you will experience a breakthrough. I can promise you that.

"When setting out on a journey, do not seek advice from someone who has never left home."

—Rumi

CHAPTER 14

COMMENCEMENT, NOT CONCLUSION

Reaching your future vision of success
and committing to the 1% Rule.

When I was about halfway through writing this book, one of my HALO team members sent me a task via email, and I responded as follows:

overworked, overwhelmed, and underperforming right now—will get back to you

That's the way my team works, and the shared language we use to give ourselves space to succeed as individuals—with the knowledge that it's how we succeed as a group. Everyone needs reflective time. HALO helps professionals succeed from anywhere on the org chart.

While most business books wrap up with a chapter titled "Conclusion" or "Final Thoughts" bringing everything to a grand crescendo, I'd suggest you think of this more like a commencement address at a graduation.

And again, that's because this is all about you and reaching your future vision of success.

Remember that letter to yourself? The one that you're going to open when you feel like you were taking two steps forward, one step back? The one that I advised you to keep handy?

I meant it.

Whenever you get frustrated, flustered, or feel like you're failing, pull it out.

Read it again.

That's why you started this journey, and why you know you can keep on going. You're crawling before you walk and walking before you run. You're building your foundation over time and creating a baseline of data. You can't just react to what you see in a snapshot of time—you need to keep going and keep growing. Before you know it, you're two years and three years in, with a robust framework of data and insights that enable you to be more analytical and predictive about business decisions—and inform you about how **REVENUE** happens at your organization.

It also helps you adapt when change happens. I can speak from my own ride in the marketing/advertising world. The days of Mad Men, cigarettes, and three-martini lunches were already a thing of the past, but Madison Avenue still had all the control in the '80s and '90s. Companies lived in a realm where they didn't necessarily have to be authentic, honest, or real. As consumers, we were the sheep that they told where to go, what to do, what to buy.

Then the dotcom era arrived. Companies that knew how to design and develop websites became the new Mad Men. The pendulum swung. And then it swung again with the advent of social media in the mid 2000s. Consumers gained even more control. By nature, we're tribal, we're seekers and finders—and the online world offered a new way to find our own answers and our own communities. And what used to work for the powers that be no longer worked.

Now, you need to be human about things. You need to think more holistically to thrive, not just survive. If you fail to maintain harmony, it comes with consequences that make it more difficult for you to sustain your business and growth going forward. If you fail to harness the value of data now and in the future, and to prepare for the surge in AI, it's going to make matters even worse.

By now, you've figured out that this book isn't just about making **REVENUE** happen, it's about making all the functions of your business move in concert, like a flywheel where each R is connected around clarity, metrics and actions. When each R moves, it's connected to the entire company accelerating together. Once you realize how integrated and interwoven all the pieces of your business are—and how they must work together in order to get to **REVENUE**—HALO is like taking a peek inside the Matrix.

You can't unsee it.

For a lot of us, entrepreneurship is ultra-energizing and motivating at the beginning. We're told to follow our passion, but then we're not provided with a framework that reduces our chance of failure. We're advised to move fast and break things, but in many cases that's counterproductive and shortsighted. We live in a day and age in which almost no effort is required to launch a website and declare yourself CEO on LinkedIn.

True entrepreneurs make the most progress when their backs are up against the wall. They don't just bask in success, they're constantly looking for ways to improve. In the good times, you're going to be good. But you need to persevere when times are rough and bad. It's like the bride and groom who get married because they're excited for the party, but they didn't listen to the vows and they're not prepared for the marriage. There's a false notion that you can just start a business and conquer the world.

I wrote this book because I want you to be successful in truth, not just in image.

The more I've achieved for my business and my clients, the more I've been able to let go of the things that first drew me to being an entrepreneur. Let's face it, it's an ego boost to say you're an entrepreneur, and if you're successful, you get the prestige, the control, and even the money that goes with it. But then I'd catch myself desiring things that were not part of my anatomy or vision of success for me and my family. HALO provides balance, a framework that keeps things in harmony—and that is my hope for you too, regardless of your aspirations and whether you're happier with a four-hour work week or a sixty-hour one.

It's been said in a million ways, but the true power of success and wealth isn't the money—it's the freedom. If you're reading this book, I'm willing to bet that freedom was part of your equation too. Financial freedom, freedom to have impact in your work, in the world. Freedom to just be yourself.

As entrepreneurs or business leaders, we all have visions of success, which is our future state. We dream about the eventual fruits of our labor, nice houses on a beach, fancy cars, vacations to the south of France, maybe even a comfortable retirement.

But then we wake up—if we're sleeping at all—to negative cash flow, pain-in-the-ass clients, dare I say pain-in-the-ass employees, and fires that only we can put out. We settle for a Pop-Tart for dinner, and a retirement account with more Lincolns than Benjamins. And then we end up thinking, "How the heck am I supposed to get from here to there?"

Every time I walk into an office, I see leaders who are overworked, overwhelmed, and underperforming. And in my head I'm thinking, "We can always make more money, but we can never make more time."

THE 1% RULE

I wake up every day with one purpose: to enable entrepreneurs like you to understand how **REVENUE** happens. You don't need an MBA to start. You don't need to travel or sit in long classes. You just need to dedicate 1% of your week to the principles laid out in these pages...such a small investment. This is what I call the 1% Rule.

I get the question often. "How do I get to be the 1%?" My only response is if you want to be in the 1% you need to invest your 1%. We've all heard coaches say, "Give it 100%" or "Give it 110%."

But that means nothing. I'm only asking you for one.

When you break it down, there are 168 hours in a week. One percent of that is 100 minutes dedicated to fixing your six R's and realigning your current state to your future state of success. It sounds simple, right? Well, because it is. But simple doesn't mean easy. I know what it takes to be that 1%, not just from what I've done in my own life, but what I've learned from working with others throughout my career. I've worked with hundreds of companies, thousands of employees, millions of their customers, and helped drive billions in revenue.

What I learned from all this is that success is not about luck. Hell, it's not even about hard work. It's about clarity, action, and measurement. If you've gotten to this page, it means that you want more from yourself, from your business, and from your employees, and you know that you're capable of more. You know that you *deserve* more. Here's the best part. The solution is right in your mirror. Like I said, you don't need an MBA. You don't need a consultant. You sure as hell don't need an overpriced business coach.

You just need HALO.

Recommended Reading

Mindset

Mindset: The New Psychology of Success, Carol Dweck

Courage Is Calling: Fortune Favors the Brave, Ryan Holiday

Creative Trespassing: How to the Spark and Joy Back Into Your Work and Life, Tania Katan

Essentialism: The Disciplined Pursuit of Less, Greg McKeown

The Almanack of Naval Ravikant: A Guide to Wealth and Happiness, Eric Jorgenson and Tim Ferriss

The Monk Who Sold His Ferrari: A Spiritual Fable About Fulfilling Your Dreams & Reaching Your Destiny, Robin Sharma

Strategy

Outliers: The Story of Success, Malcolm Gladwell

Fierce Conversations: Achieving Success at Work & in Life, One Conversation at a Time, Susan Craig Scott M.D.

So Good They Can't Ignore You: Why Skills Trump Passion in the Quest for Work You Love, Cal Newport

The Art of War, Sun Tzu

The E-Myth Revisited: Why Most Small Businesses Don't Work and What to Do About It, Michael Gerber

Better, Simpler Strategy: A Value-Based Guide to Exceptional Performance, Felix Oberholzer-Gee

Hooked: How to Build Habit-Forming Products, Nir Eyal

The 1-Page Marketing Plan, Allan Dib

Productivity

Power of Clarity, The: Unleash the True Potential of Workplace Productivity, Confidence, and Empowerment, Ann Latham

Stolen Focus: Why You Can't Pay Attention--and How to Think Deeply Again, Johann Hari

The Dip, Seth Godin

Business Made Simple: 60 Days to Master Leadership, Sales, Marketing, Execution, Management, Personal Productivity and More, Donald Miller

Metrics + Measurement

Measure What Matters: How Google, Bono, and the Gates Foundation Rock the World with OKR's, John Doerr

The Digital Mindset: What It Really Takes to Thrive in the Age of Data, Algorithms, and AI, Paul Leonardi and Tsedal Neeley

Competing on Analytics: The New Science of Winning, Thomas H. Davenport and Jeanne G. Harris

Finance

Profit First: Transform Your Business from a Cash-Eating Monster to a Money-Making Machine, Mike Michalowicz

Financial Intelligence: A Manager's Guide to Knowing What the Numbers Really Mean, Karen Berman and Joe Knight with John Case

Leadership

BE 2.0 (Beyond Entrepreneurship 2.0): Turning Your Business into an Enduring Great Company, Jim Collins and William Lazier

Vivid Vision: A Remarkable Tool for Aligning Your Business Around a Shared Vision of the Future, Cameron Herold

ABOUT THE AUTHOR

Robert Nicoletti is a seasoned strategist, driven by data and fueled by empowering businesses—from startups to Fortune 100—to create efficiencies, maximize effectiveness, and realize success in increasingly competitive marketplaces. Drawing on a rich 20-year career as a serial entrepreneur and leader in business strategy, Rob's impact and knowledge have traversed more than 40 industries. Leveraging this experience, he has successfully built companies spanning marketing and advertising, business consulting, HR, and technology. He has helped big brands stand out even more as a forerunner, including Ralph Lauren, PGA National, Humana, Ritz-Carlton, Four Seasons, and others. In leading HALO, an innovative SaaS and methodology, he's reshaping how the world works, incorporating comprehensive and visionary strategies to build a future of work that works for all.

Continuing Your HALO Journey

"If you've come this far, maybe you're willing to come a little further."

—ANDY DUFRESNE, THE SHAWSHANK REDEMPTION

Like what you've seen and experienced with HALO? If you're looking to continue on, here are a few of the different resources and pathways currently available to implement HALO and reach your own vision of success.

- Speaking Engagements

- Workshops & Retreats

- Consultation

- HALO for All (software subscription)

To learn more, contact us at *hi@haloforall.com*

www.ingramcontent.com/pod-product-compliance
Lightning Source LLC
Chambersburg PA
CBHW040918210326
41597CB00030B/5114